TRUMP TWEETS

Best of the Presidency

By Richie Richards

wet
soup
studios.

To Pepe

ISBN: 978-1-7359440-2-9 MOBI   978-7-7359440-3-6 PAPERBACK

Photographs courtesy of The White House.

www.wetsoupstudios.com

Donald J. Trump ✓ @realDonaldTrump · Jan 20, 2017

It all begins today! I will see you at 11:00 A.M. for the swearing-in. THE MOVEMENT CONTINUES - THE WORK BEGINS!

○ 29.6K   ⟲ 65.8K   ♡ 230.3K   ⬆

Donald J. Trump ✓ @realDonaldTrump · Jan 20, 2017

Today we are not merely transferring power from one Administration to another, or from one party to another – but we are transferring...

○ 5.3K   ⟲ 17.2K   ♡ 93.7K   ⬆

Donald J. Trump ✓ @realDonaldTrump · Jan 20, 2017

Replying to @realDonaldTrump

power from Washington, D.C. and giving it back to you, the American People. #InaugurationDay

○ 5.2K   ⟲ 15.6K   ♡ 77.3K   ⬆

Donald J. Trump ✓ @realDonaldTrump · Jan 20, 2017

What truly matters is not which party controls our government, but whether our government is controlled by the people.

○ 8.5K   ⟲ 39K   ♡ 155.5K   ⬆

Donald J. Trump ✓ @realDonaldTrump · Jan 20, 2017

January 20th 2017, will be remembered as the day the people became the rulers of this nation again.

○ 14.1K   ⟲ 61.1K   ♡ 195.1K   ⬆

Donald J. Trump ✓ @realDonaldTrump · Jan 20, 2017

The forgotten men and women of our country will be forgotten no longer. From this moment on, it's going to be #AmericaFirst🇺🇸

○ 6.4K   ⟲ 29.9K   ♡ 126.3K   ⬆

Donald J. Trump ✓ @realDonaldTrump · Jan 22, 2017

Peaceful protests are a hallmark of our democracy. Even if I don't always agree, I recognize the rights of people to express their views.

○ 46.4K   ⟲ 103K   ♡ 343.1K   ⬆

Donald J. Trump ✓ @realDonaldTrump · Jan 25, 2017

I will be making my Supreme Court pick on Thursday of next week. Thank you!

○ 17.3K   ⟲ 21K   ♡ 111.1K   ⬆

Donald J. Trump ✔ @realDonaldTrump · Jan 26, 2017   o o o
Ungrateful TRAITOR Chelsea Manning, who should never have been released from prison, is now calling President Obama a weak leader. Terrible!

💬 22.3K　　🔁 30.3K　　♡ 108K　　⬆

Donald J. Trump ✔ @realDonaldTrump · Jan 27, 2017   o o o
Look forward to seeing final results of VoteStand. Gregg Phillips and crew say at least 3,000,000 votes were illegal. We must do better!

💬 28.5K　　🔁 20.8K　　♡ 74.1K　　⬆

Donald J. Trump ✔ @realDonaldTrump · Jan 27, 2017   o o o
Mexico has taken advantage of the U.S. for long enough. Massive trade deficits & little help on the very weak border must change, NOW!

💬 27.4K　　🔁 30.6K　　♡ 135.4K　　⬆

Donald J. Trump ✔ @realDonaldTrump · Jan 27, 2017   o o o
The #MarchForLife is so important. To all of you marching --- you have my full support!

💬 16.9K　　🔁 42.5K　　♡ 156.4K　　⬆

Donald J. Trump ✔ @realDonaldTrump · Jan 28, 2017   o o o
The failing @nytimes has been wrong about me from the very beginning. Said I would lose the primaries, then the general election. FAKE NEWS!

💬 27.8K　　🔁 23.9K　　♡ 90.8K　　⬆

Donald J. Trump ✔ @realDonaldTrump · Jan 29, 2017   o o o
Our country needs strong borders and extreme vetting, NOW. Look what is happening all over Europe and, indeed, the world - a horrible mess!

💬 57K　　🔁 50.7K　　♡ 183.2K　　⬆

Donald J. Trump ✔ @realDonaldTrump · Jan 29, 2017   o o o
Christians in the Middle-East have been executed in large numbers. We cannot allow this horror to continue!

💬 47.5K　　🔁 62.2K　　♡ 187.9K　　⬆

Donald J. Trump ✔ @realDonaldTrump · Jan 30, 2017   o o o
If the ban were announced with a one week notice, the "bad" would rush into our country during that week. A lot of bad "dudes" out there!

💬 44.2K　　🔁 53.7K　　♡ 144.3K　　⬆

Donald J. Trump ✔ @realDonaldTrump · Jan 31, 2017   o o o
Hope you like my nomination of Judge Neil Gorsuch for the United States Supreme Court. He is a good and brilliant man, respected by all.

💬 36.6K　　🔁 32.8K　　♡ 213.6K　　⬆

Donald J. Trump ✓ @realDonaldTrump · Feb 2, 2017

If U.C. Berkeley does not allow free speech and practices violence on innocent people with a different point of view - NO FEDERAL FUNDS?

○ 37.7K   � 68.3K   ♡ 178.6K   ⬆

Donald J. Trump ✓ @realDonaldTrump · Feb 2, 2017

Iran has been formally PUT ON NOTICE for firing a ballistic missile.Should have been thankful for the terrible deal the U.S. made with them!

○ 13.7K   ↺ 24.7K   ♡ 86.6K   ⬆

Donald J. Trump ✓ @realDonaldTrump · Feb 3, 2017

Yes, Arnold Schwarzenegger did a really bad job as Governor of California and even worse on the Apprentice...but at least he tried hard!

○ 24.7K   ↺ 29.6K   ♡ 97.3K   ⬆

Donald J. Trump ✓ @realDonaldTrump · Feb 3, 2017

Iran is playing with fire - they don't appreciate how "kind" President Obama was to them. Not me!

○ 20.7K   ↺ 53.8K   ♡ 130.2K   ⬆

Donald J. Trump ✓ @realDonaldTrump · Feb 3, 2017

Professional anarchists, thugs and paid protesters are proving the point of the millions of people who voted to MAKE AMERICA GREAT AGAIN!

○ 38K   ↺ 45.7K   ♡ 142.8K   ⬆

Donald J. Trump ✓ @realDonaldTrump · Feb 3, 2017

We must keep "evil" out of our country!

○ 74.2K   ↺ 70.4K   ♡ 174.9K   ⬆

Donald J. Trump ✓ @realDonaldTrump · Feb 4, 2017

When a country is no longer able to say who can, and who cannot , come in & out, especially for reasons of safety &.security - big trouble!

○ 26.6K   ↺ 37.1K   ♡ 147.9K   ⬆

Donald J. Trump ✓ @realDonaldTrump · Feb 4, 2017

MAKE AMERICA GREAT AGAIN!

○ 49.8K   ↺ 66.8K   ♡ 215.9K   ⬆

Donald J. Trump ✓ @realDonaldTrump · Feb 5, 2017

What an amazing comeback and win by the Patriots. Tom Brady, Bob Kraft and Coach B are total winners. Wow!

○ 18.3K   ↺ 70.3K   ♡ 226.8K   ⬆

Donald J. Trump ✔ @realDonaldTrump · Feb 6, 2017

The threat from radical Islamic terrorism is very real, just look at what is happening in Europe and the Middle-East. Courts must act fast!

💬 33.9K   ⟲ 30.9K   ♡ 121.6K   ⬆

Donald J. Trump ✔ @realDonaldTrump · Feb 7, 2017

I don't know Putin, have no deals in Russia, and the haters are going crazy - yet Obama can make a deal with Iran, #1 in terror, no problem!

💬 50.9K   ⟲ 56.6K   ♡ 157.9K   ⬆

Donald J. Trump ✔ @realDonaldTrump · Feb 7, 2017

It is a disgrace that my full Cabinet is still not in place, the longest such delay in the history of our country. Obstruction by Democrats!

💬 66.6K   ⟲ 42.6K   ♡ 131.6K   ⬆

Donald J. Trump ✔ @realDonaldTrump · Feb 3, 2017

Professional anarchists, thugs and paid protesters are proving the point of the millions of people who voted to MAKE AMERICA GREAT AGAIN!

💬 38K   ⟲ 45.7K   ♡ 142.8K   ⬆

Donald J. Trump ✔ @realDonaldTrump · Feb 8, 2017

My daughter Ivanka has been treated so unfairly by @Nordstrom. She is a great person -- always pushing me to do the right thing! Terrible!

💬 86.3K   ⟲ 57.3K   ♡ 120.4K   ⬆

Donald J. Trump ✔ @realDonaldTrump · Feb 9, 2017

SEE YOU IN COURT, THE SECURITY OF OUR NATION IS AT STAKE!

💬 128.6K   ⟲ 128K   ♡ 200.6K   ⬆

Donald J. Trump ✔ @realDonaldTrump · Feb 12, 2017

The crackdown on illegal criminals is merely the keeping of my campaign promise. Gang members, drug dealers & others are being removed!

💬 24.3K   ⟲ 29.3K   ♡ 124.1K   ⬆

Donald J. Trump ✔ @realDonaldTrump · Feb 12, 2017

I know Mark Cuban well. He backed me big-time but I wasn't interested in taking all of his calls.He's not smart enough to run for president!

💬 31.2K   ⟲ 22K   ♡ 67.8K   ⬆

Donald J. Trump ✔ @realDonaldTrump · Feb 15, 2017

The real scandal here is that classified information is illegally given out by "intelligence" like candy. Very un-American!

💬 53.5K   ⟲ 39.3K   ♡ 107.4K   ⬆

Donald J. Trump ✓ @realDonaldTrump · Feb 16, 2017   ○○○
Stock market hits new high with longest winning streak in decades. Great level of confidence and optimism - even before tax plan rollout!

○ 15.6K   ↻ 22.1K   ♡ 107.5K   ↑

Donald J. Trump ✓ @realDonaldTrump · Feb 17, 2017   ○○○
The FAKE NEWS media (failing @nytimes, @NBCNews, @ABC, @CBS, @CNN) is not my enemy, it is the enemy of the American People!

○ 71.6K   ↻ 81.4K   ♡ 136.4K   ↑

Donald J. Trump ✓ @realDonaldTrump · Feb 18, 2017   ○○○
Don't believe the main stream (fake news) media.The White House is running VERY WELL. I inherited a MESS and am in the process of fixing it.

○ 57.9K   ↻ 43.7K   ♡ 155.7K   ↑

Donald J. Trump ✓ @realDonaldTrump · Feb 20, 2017   ○○○
HAPPY PRESIDENTS DAY - MAKE AMERICA GREAT AGAIN!

○ 42.3K   ↻ 46.1K   ♡ 205.2K   ↑

Donald J. Trump ✓ @realDonaldTrump · Feb 25, 2017   ○○○
The media has not reported that the National Debt in my first month went down by $12 billion vs a $200 billion increase in Obama first mo.

○ 45.2K   ↻ 63K   ♡ 169.7K   ↑

Donald J. Trump ✓ @realDonaldTrump · Feb 25, 2017   ○○○
I will not be attending the White House Correspondents' Association Dinner this year. Please wish everyone well and have a great evening!

○ 56.8K   ↻ 43.3K   ♡ 103.6K   ↑

Donald J. Trump ✓ @realDonaldTrump · Feb 25, 2017   ○○○
Congratulations to Thomas Perez, who has just been named Chairman of the DNC. I could not be happier for him, or for the Republican Party!

○ 20.4K   ↻ 29.7K   ♡ 107.2K   ↑

Donald J. Trump ✓ @realDonaldTrump · Feb 26, 2017   ○○○
Russia talk is FAKE NEWS put out by the Dems, and played up by the media, in order to mask the big election defeat and the illegal leaks!

○ 48.2K   ↻ 29.1K   ♡ 93.6K   ↑

Donald J. Trump ✓ @realDonaldTrump · Mar 2, 2017   ○○○
Since November 8th, Election Day, the Stock Market has posted $3.2 trillion in GAINS and consumer confidence is at a 15 year high. Jobs!

○ 30.7K   ↻ 35.5K   ♡ 148.3K   ↑

Donald J. Trump ✔ @realDonaldTrump · Mar 3, 2017   ⦾⦾⦾
It is so pathetic that the Dems have still not approved my full Cabinet.

💬 42.7K   ↻ 31.1K   ♡ 113.5K   ⬆️

Donald J. Trump ✔ @realDonaldTrump · Mar 3, 2017   ⦾⦾⦾
We should start an immediate investigation into @SenSchumer and his ties
to Russia and Putin. A total hypocrite!

💬 44.7K   ↻ 59K   ♡ 124.3K   ⬆️

Donald J. Trump ✔ @realDonaldTrump · Mar 4, 2017   ⦾⦾⦾
Terrible! Just found out that Obama had my "wires tapped" in Trump Tower
just before the victory. Nothing found. This is McCarthyism!

💬 46.2K   ↻ 78.1K   ♡ 138.9K   ⬆️

Donald J. Trump ✔ @realDonaldTrump · Mar 4, 2017   ⦾⦾⦾
How low has President Obama gone to tapp my phones during the very
sacred election process. This is Nixon/Watergate. Bad (or sick) guy!

💬 94.2K   ↻ 79.6K   ♡ 145.1K   ⬆️

Donald J. Trump ✔ @realDonaldTrump · Mar 5, 2017   ⦾⦾⦾
Who was it that secretly said to Russian President, "Tell Vladimir that after
the election I'll have more flexibility?" @foxandfriends

💬 32.3K   ↻ 35.4K   ♡ 104.4K   ⬆️

Donald J. Trump ✔ @realDonaldTrump · Mar 17, 2017   ⦾⦾⦾
North Korea is behaving very badly. They have been "playing" the United
States for years. China has done little to help!

💬 24.5K   ↻ 25.9K   ♡ 73.7K   ⬆️

Donald J. Trump ✔ @realDonaldTrump · Mar 18, 2017 ···
Despite what you have heard from the FAKE NEWS, I had a GREAT meeting with German Chancellor Angela Merkel. Nevertheless, Germany owes.....

💬 32.6K   ↄↄ 21.9K   ♡ 78.7K   ⬆

Donald J. Trump ✔ @realDonaldTrump · Mar 18, 2017 ···
...vast sums of money to NATO & the United States must be paid more for the powerful, and very expensive, defense it provides to Germany!

💬 28.1K   ↄↄ 19.3K   ♡ 71K   ⬆

Donald J. Trump ✔ @realDonaldTrump · Mar 26, 2017 ···
General Kelly is doing a great job at the border. Numbers are way down. Many are not even trying to come in anymore.

💬 26.2K   ↄↄ 21.8K   ♡ 90K   ⬆

Donald J. Trump ✔ @realDonaldTrump · Mar 28, 2017 ···
Big announcement by Ford today. Major investment to be made in three Michigan plants. Car companies coming back to U.S. JOBS! JOBS! JOBS!

💬 18.3K   ↄↄ 22K   ♡ 91.5K   ⬆

Donald J. Trump ✔ @realDonaldTrump · Apr 3, 2017 ···
Did Hillary Clinton ever apologize for receiving the answers to the debate? Just asking!

💬 50.4K   ↄↄ 36.6K   ♡ 88.2K   ⬆

Donald J. Trump ✔ @realDonaldTrump · Apr 10, 2017 ···
Congratulations to Justice Neil Gorsuch on his elevation to the United States Supreme Court. A great day for America! #SCOTUS

💬 9.5K   ↄↄ 13.9K   ♡ 67K   ⬆

Donald J. Trump ✓ @realDonaldTrump · Apr 12, 2017 ⋯
Jobs are returning, illegal immigration is plummeting, law, order and justice are being restored. We are truly making America great again!

💬 25.7K   🔁 29.7K   ♡ 117.1K   ↑

Donald J. Trump ✓ @realDonaldTrump · Apr 11, 2017 ⋯
North Korea is looking for trouble. If China decides to help, that would be great. If not, we will solve the problem without them! U.S.A.

💬 22.7K   🔁 63.7K   ♡ 113.4K   ↑

Donald J. Trump ✓ @realDonaldTrump · Apr 16, 2017 ⋯
Happy Easter to everyone!

💬 18.1K   🔁 36.7K   ♡ 157K   ↑

Donald J. Trump ✓ @realDonaldTrump · Apr 25, 2017 ⋯
Don't let the fake media tell you that I have changed my position on the WALL. It will get built and help stop drugs, human trafficking etc.

💬 26.4K   🔁 25.4K   ♡ 82.3K   ↑

Donald J. Trump ✓ @realDonaldTrump · May 5, 2017 ⋯
Rather than causing a big disruption in N.Y.C., I will be working out of my home in Bedminster, N.J. this weekend. Also saves country money!

💬 30K   🔁 17.6K   ♡ 55.5K   ↑

Donald J. Trump ✓ @realDonaldTrump · May 8, 2017 ⋯
Director Clapper reiterated what everybody, including the fake media already knows- there is "no evidence" of collusion w/ Russia and Trump.

💬 19.2K   🔁 16.5K   ♡ 55.2K   ↑

Donald J. Trump ✓ @realDonaldTrump · May 9, 2017 ⋯
Cryin' Chuck Schumer stated recently, "I do not have confidence in him (James Comey) any longer." Then acts so indignant. #draintheswamp

💬 37.4K   🔁 30.2K   ♡ 77.4K   ↑

Donald J. Trump ✓ @realDonaldTrump · May 11, 2017 ⋯
We finally agree on something Rosie.

> 🔴 **ROSIE** ✓ @Rosie · Dec 20, 2016
> Replying to @pricklyeater and @brianefallon
> - FIRE COMEY

💬 13.9K   🔁 39.9K   ♡ 98.6K   ↑

Donald J. Trump ✔ @realDonaldTrump · May 14, 2017

Wishing @FLOTUS Melania and all of the great mothers out there a wonderful day ahead with family and friends!

Happy #MothersDay

💬 17.7K   ↻ 19.5K   ♡ 113.7K   ⬆️

Donald J. Trump ✔ @realDonaldTrump · May 18, 2017

This is the single greatest witch hunt of a politician in American history!

💬 80.8K   ↻ 56.5K   ♡ 100.6K   ⬆️

Donald J. Trump ✔ @realDonaldTrump · May 23, 2017

All civilized nations must join together to protect human life and the sacred right of our citizens to live in safety and in peace.

💬 12.3K   ↻ 26.4K   ♡ 100.6K   ⬆️

Donald J. Trump ✔ @realDonaldTrump · May 24, 2017

Honor of a lifetime to meet His Holiness Pope Francis. I leave the Vatican more determined than ever to pursue PEACE in our world.

💬 20.4K   ↻ 24.3K   ♡ 94.4K   ⬆️

Donald J. Trump ✔ @realDonaldTrump · May 28, 2017

The Fake News Media works hard at disparaging & demeaning my use of social media because they don't want America to hear the real story!

💬 46.1K   ↻ 31.1K   ♡ 95.6K   ⬆️

Donald J. Trump ✔ @realDonaldTrump · May 29, 2017

North Korea has shown great disrespect for their neighbor, China, by shooting off yet another ballistic missile...but China is trying hard!

💬 9.5K   ↻ 11.9K   ♡ 54.2K   ⬆️

Donald J. Trump ✔ @realDonaldTrump · May 31, 2017 · · ·
Despite the constant negative press covfefe

💬   🔁   ♡   ⬆️

Donald J. Trump ✔ @realDonaldTrump · May 31, 2017 · · ·
Who can figure out the true meaning of "covfefe" ??? Enjoy!

💬 43.3K   🔁 97K   ♡ 174.8K   ⬆️

Donald J. Trump ✔ @realDonaldTrump · May 31, 2017 · · ·
Kathy Griffin should be ashamed of herself. My children, especially my 11 year old son, Barron, are having a hard time with this. Sick!

💬 60.4K   🔁 57.3K   ♡ 158.8K   ⬆️

Donald J. Trump ✔ @realDonaldTrump · Jun 1, 2017 · · ·
MAKE AMERICA GREAT AGAIN!

💬 53.3K   🔁 50.4K   ♡ 135.5K   ⬆️

Donald J. Trump ✔ @realDonaldTrump · Jun 4, 2017 · · ·
We must stop being politically correct and get down to the business of security for our people. If we don't get smart it will only get worse

💬 33.4K   🔁 68.7K   ♡ 203.7K   ⬆️

Donald J. Trump ✔ @realDonaldTrump · Jun 4, 2017 · · ·
At least 7 dead and 48 wounded in terror attack and Mayor of London says there is "no reason to be alarmed!"

💬 48.2K   🔁 65.9K   ♡ 132.8K   ⬆️

Donald J. Trump ✔ @realDonaldTrump · Jun 4, 2017 · · ·
Do you notice we are not having a gun debate right now? That's because they used knives and a truck!

💬 57.7K   🔁 60.8K   ♡ 136.3K   ⬆️

Donald J. Trump ✔ @realDonaldTrump · Jun 5, 2017 · · ·
That's right, we need a TRAVEL BAN for certain DANGEROUS countries, not some politically correct term that won't help us protect our people!

💬 30.3K   🔁 32K   ♡ 99.4K   ⬆️

Donald J. Trump ✔ @realDonaldTrump · Jun 9, 2017 · · ·
Despite so many false statements and lies, total and complete vindication...and WOW, Comey is a leaker!

💬 74.8K   🔁 44.4K   ♡ 102.8K   ⬆️

Donald J. Trump ✔ @realDonaldTrump · Jun 12, 2017   ᐧᐧᐧ

We will NEVER FORGET the victims who lost their lives one year ago today in the horrific #PulseNightClub shooting. #OrlandoUnitedDay

💬 8.3K   🔁 20K   ♡ 74.2K   ⬆️

 Donald J. Trump ✔ @realDonaldTrump · Jun 13, 2017   ᐧᐧᐧ

Well, as predicted, the 9th Circuit did it again - Ruled against the TRAVEL BAN at such a dangerous time in the history of our country. S.C.

💬 22.2K   🔁 16.7K   ♡ 54.3K   ⬆️

 Donald J. Trump ✔ @realDonaldTrump · Jun 14, 2017   ᐧᐧᐧ

Rep. Steve Scalise of Louisiana, a true friend and patriot, was badly injured but will fully recover. Our thoughts and prayers are with him.

💬 17.9K   🔁 28.2K   ♡ 117.3K   ⬆️

 Donald J. Trump ✔ @realDonaldTrump · Jun 15, 2017   ᐧᐧᐧ

Crooked H destroyed phones w/ hammer, 'bleached' emails, & had husband meet w/AG days before she was cleared- & they talk about obstruction?

💬 56.8K   🔁 56.1K   ♡ 125.4K   ⬆️

 Donald J. Trump ✔ @realDonaldTrump · Jun 16, 2017   ᐧᐧᐧ

The Fake News Media hates when I use what has turned out to be my very powerful Social Media - over 100 million people! I can go around them

💬 39.1K   🔁 30.1K   ♡ 111.2K   ⬆️

Donald J. Trump ✔ @realDonaldTrump · Jun 22, 2017   ᐧᐧᐧ

I certainly hope the Democrats do not force Nancy P out. That would be very bad for the Republican Party - and please let Cryin' Chuck stay!

💬 21.9K   🔁 25.2K   ♡ 81.2K   ⬆️

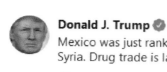

Donald J. Trump ✔ @realDonaldTrump · Jun 22, 2017   ○○○
Mexico was just ranked the second deadliest country in the world, after only
Syria. Drug trade is largely the cause. We will BUILD THE WALL!

  💬 32.6K   ⟲ 47.1K   ♡ 115.9K   ⬆

Donald J. Trump ✔ @realDonaldTrump · Jun 29, 2017   ○○○
I heard poorly rated @Morning_Joe speaks badly of me (don't watch
anymore). Then how come low I.Q. Crazy Mika, along with Psycho Joe, came..

  💬 36.5K   ⟲ 27.1K   ♡ 66.4K   ⬆

Donald J. Trump ✔ @realDonaldTrump · Jun 29, 2017   ○○○
...to Mar-a-Lago 3 nights in a row around New Year's Eve, and insisted on
joining me. She was bleeding badly from a face-lift. I said no!

  💬 79.4K   ⟲ 39.9K   ♡ 63.4K   ⬆

Donald J. Trump ✔ @realDonaldTrump · Jul 1, 2017   ○○○
Numerous states are refusing to give information to the very distinguished
VOTER FRAUD PANEL. What are they trying to hide?

  💬 61.3K   ⟲ 38.3K   ♡ 89.6K   ⬆

Donald J. Trump ✔ @realDonaldTrump · Jul 1, 2017   ○○○
My use of social media is not Presidential - it's MODERN DAY PRESIDENTIAL.
Make America Great Again!

  💬 68.6K   ⟲ 69.1K   ♡ 161.8K   ⬆

Donald J. Trump ✔ @realDonaldTrump · Jul 2, 2017   ○○○
#FraudNewsCNN #FNN

  💬 124.1K   ⟲ 462.3K   ♡ 500.7K   ⬆

Donald J. Trump ✔ @realDonaldTrump · Jul 5, 2017   ○○○

The United States made some of the worst Trade Deals in world history.Why should we continue these deals with countries that do not help us?

💬 16.3K　　　🔁 23.4K　　　♡ 105.9K　　　↑

Donald J. Trump ✔ @realDonaldTrump · Jul 12, 2017   ○○○

ISIS is on the run & will soon be wiped out of Syria & Iraq, illegal border crossings are way down (75%) & MS 13 gangs are being removed.

💬 14.3K　　　🔁 25.6K　　　♡ 104.4K　　　↑

Donald J. Trump ✔ @realDonaldTrump · Jul 16, 2017   ○○○

HillaryClinton can illegally get the questions to the Debate & delete 33,000 emails but my son Don is being scorned by the Fake News Media?

💬 47.1K　　　🔁 37.4K　　　♡ 117.2K　　　↑

Donald J. Trump ✔ @realDonaldTrump · Jul 17, 2017   ○○○

Most politicians would have gone to a meeting like the one Don jr attended in order to get info on an opponent. That's politics!

💬 60K　　　🔁 27.6K　　　♡ 84.1K　　　↑

Donald J. Trump ✔ @realDonaldTrump · Jul 24, 2017   ○○○

Drain the Swamp should be changed to Drain the Sewer - it's actually much worse than anyone ever thought, and it begins with the Fake News!

💬 31.3K　　　🔁 32K　　　♡ 96.2K　　　↑

Donald J. Trump ✔ @realDonaldTrump · Jul 26, 2017   ○○○

After consultation with my Generals and military experts, please be advised that the United States Government will not accept or allow......

💬 23.5K　　　🔁 44.3K　　　♡ 101.5K　　　↑

Donald J. Trump ✔ @realDonaldTrump · Jul 26, 2017   ○○○

....Transgender individuals to serve in any capacity in the U.S. Military. Our military must be focused on decisive and overwhelming.....

💬 40.5K　　　🔁 64.1K　　　♡ 110.5K　　　↑

Donald J. Trump ✔ @realDonaldTrump · Jul 26, 2017   ○○○

....victory and cannot be burdened with the tremendous medical costs and disruption that transgender in the military would entail. Thank you

💬 65.1K　　　🔁 64.6K　　　♡ 114.3K　　　↑

Donald J. Trump ✔ @realDonaldTrump · Jul 26, 2017   ○○○

IN AMERICA WE DON'T WORSHIP GOVERNMENT - WE WORSHIP GOD!🎥
45.wh.gov/POTUSInsta

💬 74.4K　　　🔁 73.2K　　　♡ 110.8K　　　↑

Donald J. Trump ✔ @realDonaldTrump · Jul 27, 2017

Come on Republican Senators, you can do it on Healthcare. After 7 years, this is your chance to shine! Don't let the American people down!

💬 22.8K   🔁 20.2K   ♡ 76.7K   ⬆️

Donald J. Trump ✔ @realDonaldTrump · Aug 2, 2017

I love the White House, one of the most beautiful buildings (homes) I have ever seen. But Fake News said I called it a dump - TOTALLY UNTRUE

💬 39.6K   🔁 32.8K   ♡ 113.9K   ⬆️

Donald J. Trump ✔ @realDonaldTrump · Aug 7, 2017

I think Senator Blumenthal should take a nice long vacation in Vietnam, where he lied about his service, so he can at least say he was there

💬 45.7K   🔁 32.2K   ♡ 94.1K   ⬆️

Donald J. Trump ✔ @realDonaldTrump · Aug 12, 2017

We must remember this truth: No matter our color, creed, religion or political party, we are ALL AMERICANS FIRST.

we must remember this truth: No matter our color, c

💬 26K   🔁 33K   ♡ 94.3K   ⬆️

Donald J. Trump ✔ @realDonaldTrump · Aug 12, 2017

We ALL must be united & condemn all that hate stands for. There is no place for this kind of violence in America. Lets come together as one!

💬 59.9K   🔁 72K   ♡ 162.7K   ⬆️

Donald J. Trump ✔ @realDonaldTrump · Aug 12, 2017

Deepest condolences to the families & fellow officers of the VA State Police who died today. You're all among the best this nation produces.

💬 18.1K   🔁 23.5K   ♡ 105.8K   ⬆️

Donald J. Trump ✓ @realDonaldTrump · Aug 12, 2017

Condolences to the family of the young woman killed today, and best regards to all of those injured, in Charlottesville, Virginia. So sad!

💬 56.8K   🔁 31.3K   ♡ 92.4K   ⬆️

Donald J. Trump ✓ @realDonaldTrump · Aug 16, 2017

MAKE AMERICA GREAT AGAIN!

💬 51.8K   🔁 56K   ♡ 141.9K   ⬆️

Donald J. Trump ✓ @realDonaldTrump · Aug 17, 2017

Sad to see the history and culture of our great country being ripped apart with the removal of our beautiful statues and monuments. You.....

💬 41.5K   🔁 45.4K   ♡ 110.2K   ⬆️

Donald J. Trump ✓ @realDonaldTrump · Aug 17, 2017

...can't change history, but you can learn from it. Robert E Lee, Stonewall Jackson - who's next, Washington, Jefferson? So foolish! Also...

💬 37.4K   🔁 35K   ♡ 111.9K   ⬆️

Donald J. Trump ✓ @realDonaldTrump · Aug 17, 2017

...the beauty that is being taken out of our cities, towns and parks will be greatly missed and never able to be comparably replaced!

💬 47.9K   🔁 31K   ♡ 92.3K   ⬆️

Donald J. Trump ✓ @realDonaldTrump · Aug 19, 2017

I want to thank Steve Bannon for his service. He came to the campaign during my run against Crooked Hillary Clinton - it was great! Thanks S

💬 28.1K   🔁 26K   ♡ 97.9K   ⬆️

Donald J. Trump ✓ @realDonaldTrump · Aug 19, 2017

Our great country has been divided for decades. Sometimes you need protest in order to heal, & we will heal, & be stronger than ever before!

💬 32.6K   🔁 28K   ♡ 119.2K   ⬆️

Donald J. Trump ✓ @realDonaldTrump · Aug 19, 2017

I want to applaud the many protestors in Boston who are speaking out against bigotry and hate. Our country will soon come together as one!

💬 46.4K   🔁 36K   ♡ 131.8K   ⬆️

Donald J. Trump ✓ @realDonaldTrump · Sep 3, 2017

The United States is considering, in addition to other options, stopping all trade with any country doing business with North Korea.

💬 31.8K   🔁 47.1K   ♡ 140.9K   ⬆️

Donald J. Trump ✔ @realDonaldTrump · Sep 15, 2017

The travel ban into the United States should be far larger, tougher and more specific-but stupidly, that would not be politically correct!

◯ 18.5K   ⟲ 22.8K   ♡ 86.7K   ⬆

Donald J. Trump ✔ @realDonaldTrump · Sep 15, 2017

CHAIN MIGRATION cannot be allowed to be part of any legislation on Immigration!

◯ 10.5K   ⟲ 16.9K   ♡ 62.4K   ⬆

Donald J. Trump ✔ @realDonaldTrump · Sep 17, 2017

I spoke with President Moon of South Korea last night. Asked him how Rocket Man is doing. Long gas lines forming in North Korea. Too bad!

◯ 22.2K   ⟲ 48.3K   ♡ 121.6K   ⬆

Donald J. Trump ✔ @realDonaldTrump · Sep 19, 2017

The▪has great strength & patience, but if it is forced to defend itself or its allies, we will have no choice but to totally destroy #NoKo.

◯ 14.8K   ⟲ 23.1K   ♡ 69.3K   ⬆

Donald J. Trump ✔ @realDonaldTrump · Sep 22, 2017

Kim Jong Un of North Korea, who is obviously a madman who doesn't mind starving or killing his people, will be tested like never before!

◯ 27.1K   ⟲ 45.7K   ♡ 108K   ⬆

Donald J. Trump ✔ @realDonaldTrump · Sep 23, 2017

If a player wants the privilege of making millions of dollars in the NFL,or other leagues, he or she should not be allowed to disrespect....

◯ 45.3K   ⟲ 54.1K   ♡ 153.5K   ⬆

Donald J. Trump ✔ @realDonaldTrump · Sep 23, 2017
...our Great American Flag (or Country) and should stand for the National Anthem. If not, YOU'RE FIRED. Find something else to do!

💬 53.8K　　🔁 48.1K　　♡ 134K　　⬆️

Donald J. Trump ✔ @realDonaldTrump · Sep 25, 2017
So proud of NASCAR and its supporters and fans. They won't put up with disrespecting our Country or our Flag - they said it loud and clear!

💬 26.8K　　🔁 36.9K　　♡ 145.5K　　⬆️

Donald J. Trump ✔ @realDonaldTrump · Sep 25, 2017
The issue of kneeling has nothing to do with race. It is about respect for our Country, Flag and National Anthem. NFL must respect this!

💬 49.1K　　🔁 57.5K　　♡ 173.9K　　⬆️

Donald J. Trump ✔ @realDonaldTrump · Oct 1, 2017
Being nice to Rocket Man hasn't worked in 25 years, why would it work now? Clinton failed, Bush failed, and Obama failed. I won't fail.

💬 64.4K　　🔁 59.3K　　♡ 157.7K　　⬆️

Donald J. Trump ✔ @realDonaldTrump · Oct 2, 2017
My warmest condolences and sympathies to the victims and families of the terrible Las Vegas shooting. God bless you!

💬 53.6K　　🔁 74.6K　　♡ 269.3K　　⬆️

Donald J. Trump ✔ @realDonaldTrump · Oct 3, 2017
It is a "miracle" how fast the Las Vegas Metropolitan Police were able to find the demented shooter and stop him from even more killing!

💬 21.5K　　🔁 19.7K　　♡ 87.6K　　⬆️

Donald J. Trump ✔ @realDonaldTrump · Oct 5, 2017
Stock Market hits an ALL-TIME high! Unemployment lowest in 16 years! Business and manufacturing enthusiasm at highest level in decades!

💬 27.8K　　🔁 34.2K　　♡ 132.5K　　⬆️

Donald J. Trump ✔ @realDonaldTrump · Oct 10, 2017
Why is the NFL getting massive tax breaks while at the same time disrespecting our Anthem, Flag and Country? Change tax law!

💬 35.4K　　🔁 33.3K　　♡ 115.1K　　⬆️

Donald J. Trump ✔ @realDonaldTrump · Oct 16, 2017
I was recently asked if Crooked Hillary Clinton is going to run in 2020? My answer was, "I hope so!"

💬 51K　　🔁 36.7K　　♡ 123.9K　　⬆️

Donald J. Trump ✔ @realDonaldTrump · Oct 21, 2017

Subject to the receipt of further information, I will be allowing, as President, the long blocked and classified JFK FILES to be opened.

💬 34.9K　　🔁 75.2K　　♡ 175.5K　　⬆️

Donald J. Trump ✔ @realDonaldTrump · Oct 28, 2017

Just read the nice remarks by President Jimmy Carter about me and how badly I am treated by the press (Fake News). Thank you Mr. President!

💬 21.4K　　🔁 21K　　♡ 111.4K　　⬆️

Donald J. Trump ✔ @realDonaldTrump · Oct 28, 2017

While not at all presidential I must point out that the Sloppy Michael Moore Show on Broadway was a TOTAL BOMB and was forced to close. Sad!

💬 44.1K　　🔁 31K　　♡ 94.2K　　⬆️

Donald J. Trump ✔ @realDonaldTrump · Oct 31, 2017

I have just ordered Homeland Security to step up our already Extreme Vetting Program. Being politically correct is fine, but not for this!

💬 35.7K　　🔁 36.2K　　♡ 122K　　⬆️

Donald J. Trump ✔ @realDonaldTrump · Nov 1, 2017

NYC terrorist was happy as he asked to hang ISIS flag in his hospital room. He killed 8 people, badly injured 12. SHOULD GET DEATH PENALTY!

💬 30.8K　　🔁 41.3K　　♡ 144.6K　　⬆️

Donald J. Trump ✔ @realDonaldTrump · Nov 9, 2017

I don't blame China, I blame the incompetence of past Admins for allowing China to take advantage of the U.S. on trade leading up to a point where the U.S. is losing $100's of billions. How can you blame China for taking advantage of people that had no clue? I would've done same!

💬 27.7K　　🔁 30.3K　　♡ 112.5K　　⬆️

Donald J. Trump ✔ @realDonaldTrump · Nov 11, 2017

Met with President Putin of Russia who was at #APEC meetings. Good discussions on Syria. Hope for his help to solve, along with China the dangerous North Korea crisis. Progress being made.

💬 8.7K　　🔁 12.8K　　♡ 61.5K　　⬆️

Donald J. Trump ✔ @realDonaldTrump · Nov 11, 2017

When will all the haters and fools out there realize that having a good relationship with Russia is a good thing, not a bad thing. There always playing politics - bad for our country. I want to solve North Korea, Syria, Ukraine, terrorism, and Russia can greatly help!

💬 54.4K　　🔁 50.9K　　♡ 129.9K　　⬆️

Donald J. Trump ✓ @realDonaldTrump · Nov 11, 2017   ooo
Why would Kim Jong-un insult me by calling me "old," when I would NEVER call him "short and fat?" Oh well, I try so hard to be his friend - and maybe someday that will happen!

💬 114.1K   ↻ 416.2K   ♡ 531.7K   ⬆

Donald J. Trump ✓ @realDonaldTrump · Nov 16, 2017   ooo
The Al Frankenstien picture is really bad, speaks a thousand words. Where do his hands go in pictures 2, 3, 4, 5 & 6 while she sleeps? .....

💬 86.2K   ↻ 38.4K   ♡ 69.2K   ⬆

Donald J. Trump ✓ @realDonaldTrump · Nov 22, 2017   ooo
It wasn't the White House, it wasn't the State Department, it wasn't father LaVar's so-called people on the ground in China that got his son out of a long term prison sentence - IT WAS ME. Too bad! LaVar is just a poor man's version of Don King, but without the hair. Just think..

💬 47.4K   ↻ 52.5K   ♡ 103.6K   ⬆

Donald J. Trump ✓ @realDonaldTrump · Nov 22, 2017   ooo
...LaVar, you could have spent the next 5 to 10 years during Thanksgiving with your son in China, but no NBA contract to support you. But remember LaVar, shoplifting is NOT a little thing. It's a really big deal, especially in China. Ungrateful fool!

💬 35.5K   ↻ 45K   ♡ 133.5K   ⬆

Donald J. Trump ✓ @realDonaldTrump · Nov 24, 2017   ooo
Horrible and cowardly terrorist attack on innocent and defenseless worshipers in Egypt. The world cannot tolerate terrorism, we must defeat them militarily and discredit the extremist ideology that forms the basis of their existence!

Donald J. Trump ✓ @realDonaldTrump · Nov 24, 2017   ooo
Time Magazine called to say that I was PROBABLY going to be named "Man (Person) of the Year," like last year, but I would have to agree to an interview and a major photo shoot. I said probably is no good and took a pass. Thanks anyway!

💬 102K   ↻ 74.3K   ♡ 137.5K   ⬆

Donald J. Trump ✓ @realDonaldTrump · Nov 30, 2017   ooo
A disgraceful verdict in the Kate Steinle case! No wonder the people of our Country are so angry with Illegal Immigration.

💬 27.6K   ↻ 37.9K   ♡ 128K   ⬆

Donald J. Trump ✔ @realDonaldTrump · Dec 2, 2017   ০০০

I had to fire General Flynn because he lied to the Vice President and the FBI. He has pled guilty to those lies. It is a shame because his actions during the transition were lawful. There was nothing to hide!

🗨 65.3K   ⟲ 50.2K   ♡ 99.5K   ⬆

 Donald J. Trump ✔ @realDonaldTrump · Dec 6, 2017   ০০০

MAKE AMERICA GREAT AGAIN!

🗨 47.5K   ⟲ 46K   ♡ 156K   ⬆

Donald J. Trump ✔ @realDonaldTrump · Dec 6, 2017   ০০০

I have determined that it is time to officially recognize Jerusalem as the capital of Israel. I am also directing the State Department to begin preparation to move the American Embassy from Tel Aviv to Jerusalem...

1:12 4M views

🗨 48.9K   ⟲ 39.9K   ♡ 112.3K   ⬆

 Donald J. Trump ✔ @realDonaldTrump · Dec 11, 2017   ০০০

Another false story, this time in the Failing @nytimes, that I watch 4-8 hours of television a day - Wrong! Also, I seldom, if ever, watch CNN or MSNBC, both of which I consider Fake News. I never watch Don Lemon, who I once called the "dumbest man on television!" Bad Reporting.

🗨 62.9K   ⟲ 36.1K   ♡ 112.4K   ⬆

 Donald J. Trump ✔ @realDonaldTrump · Dec 12, 2017   ০০০

Despite thousands of hours wasted and many millions of dollars spent, the Democrats have been unable to show any collusion with Russia - so now they are moving on to the false accusations and fabricated stories of women who I don't know and/or have never met. FAKE NEWS!

🗨 49K   ⟲ 35.1K   ♡ 121K   ⬆

Donald J. Trump ✔ @realDonaldTrump · Dec 19, 2017   ⊙⊙⊙

DOW RISES 5000 POINTS ON THE YEAR FOR THE FIRST TIME EVER - MAKE AMERICA GREAT AGAIN!

💬 13.5K   ⟲ 20.7K   ♡ 94.8K   ⬆

Donald J. Trump ✔ @realDonaldTrump · Dec 22, 2017   ⊙⊙⊙

Remember, the most hated part of ObamaCare is the Individual Mandate, which is being terminated under our just signed Tax Cut Bill.

💬 24.6K   ⟲ 22.3K   ♡ 99.6K   ⬆

Donald J. Trump ✔ @realDonaldTrump · Dec 24, 2017   ⊙⊙⊙

People are proud to be saying Merry Christmas again. I am proud to have led the charge against the assault of our cherished and beautiful phrase. MERRY CHRISTMAS!!!!!

💬 89.2K   ⟲ 71.3K   ♡ 194.7K   ⬆

Donald J. Trump ✔ @realDonaldTrump · Dec 25, 2017   ⊙⊙⊙

I hope everyone is having a great Christmas, then tomorrow it's back to work in order to Make America Great Again (which is happening faster than anyone anticipated)!

💬 35.2K   ⟲ 30.6K   ♡ 167.5K   ⬆

Donald J. Trump ✔ @realDonaldTrump · Dec 28, 2017   ⊙⊙⊙

In the East, it could be the COLDEST New Year's Eve on record. Perhaps we could use a little bit of that good old Global Warming that our Country, but not other countries, was going to pay TRILLIONS OF DOLLARS to protect against. Bundle up!

💬 121K   ⟲ 179.9K   ♡ 172.5K   ⬆

Donald J. Trump ✔ @realDonaldTrump · Dec 30, 2017   ⊙⊙⊙

I use Social Media not because I like to, but because it is the only way to fight a VERY dishonest and unfair "press," now often referred to as Fake News Media. Phony and non-existent "sources" are being used more often than ever. Many stories & reports a pure fiction!

💬 50.2K   ⟲ 52K   ♡ 176.8K   ⬆

Donald J. Trump ✔ @realDonaldTrump · Jan 1, 2018   ⊙⊙⊙

The United States has foolishly given Pakistan more than 33 billion dollars in aid over the last 15 years, and they have given us nothing but lies & deceit, thinking of our leaders as fools. They give safe haven to the terrorists we hunt in Afghanistan, with little help. No more!

💬 50.9K   ⟲ 100.8K   ♡ 261.8K   ⬆

Donald J. Trump ✔ @realDonaldTrump · Jan 2, 2018   000

North Korean Leader Kim Jong Un just stated that the "Nuclear Button is on his desk at all times." Will someone from his depleted and food starved regime please inform him that I too have a Nuclear Button, but it is a much bigger & more powerful one than his, and my Button works!

💬 137K   ⟲ 380.7K   ♡ 427.3K   ⬆️

Donald J. Trump ✔ @realDonaldTrump · Jan 2, 2018   000

I will be announcing THE MOST DISHONEST & CORRUPT MEDIA AWARDS OF THE YEAR on Monday at 5:00 o'clock. Subjects will cover Dishonesty & Bad Reporting in various categories from the Fake News Media. Stay tuned!

💬 70.7K   ⟲ 81.2K   ♡ 162.7K   ⬆️

Donald J. Trump ✔ @realDonaldTrump · Jan 4, 2018   000

As Americans, you need identification, sometimes in a very strong and accurate form, for almost everything you do.....except when it comes to the most important thing, VOTING for the people that run your country. Push hard for Voter Identification!

💬 21.6K   ⟲ 35.3K   ♡ 128.8K   ⬆️

Donald J. Trump ✔ @realDonaldTrump · Jan 4, 2018   000

MAKING AMERICA GREAT AGAIN!

💬 15.5K   ⟲ 19.2K   ♡ 77.8K   ⬆️

Donald J. Trump ✔ @realDonaldTrump · Jan 6, 2018   000

Now that Russian collusion, after one year of intense study, has proven to be a total hoax on the American public, the Democrats and their lapdogs, the Fake News Mainstream Media, are taking out the old Ronald Reagan playbook and screaming mental stability and intelligence.....

💬 34.7K   ⟲ 31.7K   ♡ 122.6K   ⬆️

Donald J. Trump ✔ @realDonaldTrump · Jan 6, 2018 ₀₀₀

....Actually, throughout my life, my two greatest assets have been mental stability and being, like, really smart. Crooked Hillary Clinton also played these cards very hard and, as everyone knows, went down in flames. I went from VERY successful businessman, to top T.V. Star.....

💬 58.9K   ↻ 71.6K   ♡ 111.8K   ⬆

Donald J. Trump ✔ @realDonaldTrump · Jan 6, 2018 ₀₀₀

....to President of the United States (on my first try). I think that would qualify as not smart, but genius....and a very stable genius at that!

💬 92.1K   ↻ 53.6K   ♡ 117.8K   ⬆

Donald J. Trump ✔ @realDonaldTrump · Jan 13, 2018 ₀₀₀

AMERICA FIRST!

💬 32.4K   ↻ 33.5K   ♡ 125.2K   ⬆

Donald J. Trump ✔ @realDonaldTrump · Jan 14, 2018 ₀₀₀

I, as President, want people coming into our Country who are going to help us become strong and great again, people coming in through a system based on MERIT. No more Lotteries! #AMERICA FIRST

💬 34.2K   ↻ 35.6K   ♡ 132.7K   ⬆

Donald J. Trump ✔ @realDonaldTrump · Jan 17, 2018 ₀₀₀

And the FAKE NEWS winners are...

The Highly Anticipated 2017 Fake News Awards
2017 has been a year of unrelenting bias, unfair news coverage, and even downright fake news.
🔗 gop.com

💬 36.5K   ↻ 42.6K   ♡ 91.3K   ⬆

Donald J. Trump ✔ @realDonaldTrump · Jan 20, 2018

Beautiful weather all over our great country, a perfect day for all Women to March. Get out there now to celebrate the historic milestones and unprecedented economic success and wealth creation that has taken place over the last 12 months. Lowest female unemployment in 18 years!

💬 70.7K   🔁 65K   ♡ 173.3K   ⬆

Donald J. Trump ✔ @realDonaldTrump · Jan 20, 2018

The Trump Administration has terminated more UNNECESSARY Regulation, in just twelve months, than any other Administration has terminated during their full term in office, no matter what the length. The good news is, THERE IS MUCH MORE TO COME!

💬 26.9K   🔁 27.6K   ♡ 129.2K   ⬆

Donald J. Trump ✔ @realDonaldTrump · Jan 27, 2018

I have offered DACA a wonderful deal, including a doubling in the number of recipients & a twelve year pathway to citizenship, for two reasons: (1) Because the Republicans want to fix a long time terrible problem. (2) To show that Democrats do not want to solve DACA, only use it!

💬 28.9K   🔁 40.7K   ♡ 146.6K   ⬆

Donald J. Trump ✔ @realDonaldTrump · Jan 27, 2018

Democrats are not interested in Border Safety & Security or in the funding and rebuilding of our Military. They are only interested in Obstruction!

💬 31.8K   🔁 31K   ♡ 130.6K   ⬆

Donald J. Trump ✔ @realDonaldTrump · Jan 28, 2018

Somebody please inform Jay-Z that because of my policies, Black Unemployment has just been reported to be at the LOWEST RATE EVER RECORDED!

💬 59.6K   🔁 72.1K   ♡ 199.7K   ⬆

Donald J. Trump ✔ @realDonaldTrump · Feb 1, 2018

Thank you for all of the nice compliments and reviews on the State of the Union speech. 45.6 million people watched, the highest number in history. @FoxNews beat every other Network, for the first time ever, with 11.7 million people tuning in. Delivered from the heart!

💬 71K   🔁 38.3K   ♡ 154.4K   ⬆

Donald J. Trump ✔ @realDonaldTrump · Feb 5, 2018

Representative Devin Nunes, a man of tremendous courage and grit, may someday be recognized as a Great American Hero for what he has exposed and what he has had to endure!

💬 46.9K   🔁 33.2K   ♡ 109.7K   ⬆

Donald J. Trump ✔ @realDonaldTrump · Feb 6, 2018 ₀₀₀

HAPPY BIRTHDAY to our 40th President of the United States of America, Ronald Reagan!

💬 17.7K   🔁 28.4K   ♡ 153K   ⬆️

 Donald J. Trump ✔ @realDonaldTrump · Feb 14, 2018 ₀₀₀

My prayers and condolences to the families of the victims of the terrible Florida shooting. No child, teacher or anyone else should ever feel unsafe in an American school.

💬 66.9K   🔁 53.3K   ♡ 148.1K   ⬆️

 Donald J. Trump ✔ @realDonaldTrump · Feb 18, 2018 ₀₀₀

Never gotten over the fact that Obama was able to send $1.7 Billion Dollars in CASH to Iran and nobody in Congress, the FBI or Justice called for an investigation!

💬 27.8K   🔁 38.3K   ♡ 107.5K   ⬆️

 Donald J. Trump ✔ @realDonaldTrump · Feb 18, 2018 ₀₀₀

I never said Russia did not meddle in the election, I said "it may be Russia, or China or another country or group, or it may be a 400 pound genius sitting in bed and playing with his computer." The Russian "hoax" was that the Trump campaign colluded with Russia - it never did!

💬 37.3K   🔁 30.9K   ♡ 105.8K   ⬆️

 Donald J. Trump ✔ @realDonaldTrump · Feb 19, 2018 ₀₀₀

Have a great, but very reflective, President's Day!

💬 50.6K   🔁 25.8K   ♡ 120.7K   ⬆️

Donald J. Trump ✔ @realDonaldTrump · Feb 27, 2018

WITCH HUNT!

💬 54.9K   🔁 34K   ❤️ 77.2K   ⬆️

Donald J. Trump ✔ @realDonaldTrump · Mar 2, 2018

Alec Baldwin, whose dying mediocre career was saved by his terrible impersonation of me on SNL, now says playing me was agony. Alec, it was agony for those who were forced to watch. Bring back Darrell Hammond, funnier and a far greater talent!

💬 45.1K   🔁 33.3K   ❤️ 116.5K   ⬆️

Donald J. Trump ✔ @realDonaldTrump · Mar 6, 2018

Lowest rated Oscars in HISTORY. Problem is, we don't have Stars anymore - except your President (just kidding, of course)!

💬 41.9K   🔁 75.5K   ❤️ 178K   ⬆️

Donald J. Trump ✔ @realDonaldTrump · Mar 12, 2018

THE HOUSE INTELLIGENCE COMMITTEE HAS, AFTER A 14 MONTH LONG IN-DEPTH INVESTIGATION, FOUND NO EVIDENCE OF COLLUSION OR COORDINATION BETWEEN THE TRUMP CAMPAIGN AND RUSSIA TO INFLUENCE THE 2016 PRESIDENTIAL ELECTION.

💬 68.8K   🔁 47.4K   ❤️ 134.3K   ⬆️

Donald J. Trump ✔ @realDonaldTrump · Mar 13, 2018

Mike Pompeo, Director of the CIA, will become our new Secretary of State. He will do a fantastic job! Thank you to Rex Tillerson for his service! Gina Haspel will become the new Director of the CIA, and the first woman so chosen. Congratulations to all!

💬 36.5K   🔁 44K   ❤️ 103.3K   ⬆️

Donald J. Trump ✔ @realDonaldTrump · Mar 17, 2018

Andrew McCabe FIRED, a great day for the hard working men and women of the FBI - A great day for Democracy. Sanctimonious James Comey was his boss and made McCabe look like a choirboy. He knew all about the lies and corruption going on at the highest levels of the FBI!

💬 89.3K   🔁 50.1K   ❤️ 135.7K   ⬆️

Donald J. Trump ✔ @realDonaldTrump · Mar 20, 2018

Our Nation was founded by farmers. Our independence was won by farmers. And our continent was tamed by farmers. Our farmers always lead the way -- we are PROUD of them, and we are DELIVERING for them! #NationalAgricultureDay

💬 28.1K   🔁 31K   ❤️ 118.4K   ⬆️

Donald J. Trump ✓ @realDonaldTrump · Mar 22, 2018

Crazy Joe Biden is trying to act like a tough guy. Actually, he is weak, both mentally and physically, and yet he threatens me, for the second time, with physical assault. He doesn't know me, but he would go down fast and hard, crying all the way. Don't threaten people Joe!

💬 90.4K   🔁 134.6K   ♡ 215K   ⬆️

Donald J. Trump ✓ @realDonaldTrump · Mar 28, 2018

THE SECOND AMENDMENT WILL NEVER BE REPEALED! As much as Democrats would like to see this happen, and despite the words yesterday of former Supreme Court Justice Stevens, NO WAY. We need more Republicans in 2018 and must ALWAYS hold the Supreme Court!

💬 34.3K   🔁 54.2K   ♡ 161.4K   ⬆️

Donald J. Trump ✓ @realDonaldTrump · Apr 1, 2018

Mexico is doing very little, if not NOTHING, at stopping people from flowing into Mexico through their Southern Border, and then into the U.S. They laugh at our dumb immigration laws. They must stop the big drug and people flows, or I will stop their cash cow, NAFTA. NEED WALL!

💬 30.2K   🔁 31.5K   ♡ 104.3K   ⬆️

Donald J. Trump ✓ @realDonaldTrump · Apr 11, 2018

Russia vows to shoot down any and all missiles fired at Syria. Get ready Russia, because they will be coming, nice and new and "smart!" You shouldn't be partners with a Gas Killing Animal who kills his people and enjoys it!

💬 57.1K   🔁 93.6K   ♡ 145.5K   ⬆️

Donald J. Trump ✓ @realDonaldTrump · Apr 12, 2018

Never said when an attack on Syria would take place. Could be very soon or not so soon at all! In any event, the United States, under my Administration, has done a great job of ridding the region of ISIS. Where is our "Thank you America?"

💬 43.5K   🔁 30.9K   ♡ 95.2K   ⬆️

Donald J. Trump ✓ @realDonaldTrump · Apr 13, 2018

James Comey is a proven LEAKER & LIAR. Virtually everyone in Washington thought he should be fired for the terrible job he did-until he was, in fact, fired. He leaked CLASSIFIED information, for which he should be prosecuted. He lied to Congress under OATH. He is a weak and.....

💬 43.6K   🔁 32.4K   ♡ 105K   ⬆️

Donald J. Trump ✓ @realDonaldTrump · Apr 13, 2018 ⚬⚬⚬

....untruthful slime ball who was, as time has proven, a terrible Director of the FBI. His handling of the Crooked Hillary Clinton case, and the events surrounding it, will go down as one of the worst "botch jobs" of history. It was my great honor to fire James Comey!

💬 63.7K　　🔁 36.4K　　♡ 117.7K　　⬆️

Donald J. Trump ✓ @realDonaldTrump · Apr 15, 2018 ⚬⚬⚬

Slippery James Comey, a man who always ends up badly and out of whack (he is not smart!), will go down as the WORST FBI Director in history, by far!

💬 43.2K　　🔁 22.7K　　♡ 81.9K　　⬆️

Donald J. Trump ✓ @realDonaldTrump · Apr 20, 2018 ⚬⚬⚬

A message from Kim Jong Un: "North Korea will stop nuclear tests and launches of intercontinental ballistic missiles."
Also will "Shut down a nuclear test site in the country's Northern Side to prove the vow to suspend nuclear tests." Progress being made for all!

💬 12.6K　　🔁 27.9K　　♡ 119.7K　　⬆️

Donald J. Trump ✓ @realDonaldTrump · Apr 25, 2018 ⚬⚬⚬

Thank you Kanye, very cool!

> ⚫ **ye** ✓ @kanyewest · Apr 25, 2018
>
> You don't have to agree with trump but the mob can't make me not love him. We are both dragon energy. He is my brother. I love everyone. I don't agree with everything anyone does. That's what makes us individuals. And we have the right to independent thought.

💬 19.4K　　🔁 113.2K　　♡ 316.3K　　⬆️

Donald J. Trump ✓ @realDonaldTrump · Apr 27, 2018 ⚬⚬⚬

KOREAN WAR TO END! The United States, and all of its GREAT people, should be very proud of what is now taking place in Korea!

💬 11K　　🔁 33.9K　　♡ 111.6K　　⬆️

Donald J. Trump ✓ @realDonaldTrump · May 4, 2018 ⚬⚬⚬

JUST OUT: 3.9% Unemployment. 4% is Broken! In the meantime, WITCH HUNT!

💬 24.2K　　🔁 27.2K　　♡ 114.7K　　⬆️

Donald J. Trump ✓ @realDonaldTrump · May 8, 2018 ⚬⚬⚬

John Kerry can't get over the fact that he had his chance and blew it! Stay away from negotiations John, you are hurting your country!

💬 24.3K　　🔁 29.4K　　♡ 114K　　⬆️

Donald J. Trump ✓ @realDonaldTrump · May 10, 2018   ooo

On behalf of the American people, WELCOME HOME!

💬 14.9K   ⟲ 44.4K   ♡ 162.2K   ↥

Donald J. Trump ✓ @realDonaldTrump · May 10, 2018   ooo

Five Most Wanted leaders of ISIS just captured!

💬 15.7K   ⟲ 61.2K   ♡ 256.8K   ↥

Donald J. Trump ✓ @realDonaldTrump · May 11, 2018   ooo

Big week next week when the American Embassy in Israel will be moved to Jerusalem. Congratulations to all!

💬 12.8K   ⟲ 26.9K   ♡ 122.1K   ↥

Donald J. Trump ✓ @realDonaldTrump · May 12, 2018   ooo

North Korea has announced that they will dismantle Nuclear Test Site this month, ahead of the big Summit Meeting on June 12th. Thank you, a very smart and gracious gesture!

💬 13.9K   ⟲ 29.9K   ♡ 137.2K   ↥

Donald J. Trump ✓ @realDonaldTrump · May 18, 2018   ooo

Fake News Media had me calling Immigrants, or Illegal Immigrants, "Animals." Wrong! They were begrudgingly forced to withdraw their stories. I referred to MS 13 Gang Members as "Animals," a big difference - and so true. Fake News got it purposely wrong, as usual!

💬 22K   ⟲ 37.2K   ♡ 134.1K   ↥

Donald J. Trump ✓ @realDonaldTrump · May 24, 2018   ooo

Clapper has now admitted that there was Spying in my campaign. Large dollars were paid to the Spy, far beyond normal. Starting to look like one of the biggest political scandals in U.S. history. SPYGATE - a terrible thing!

💬 36.9K   ⟲ 29.5K   ♡ 91.6K   ↥

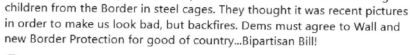

Donald J. Trump ✔ @realDonaldTrump · May 27, 2018   ○○○
Why didn't President Obama do something about the so-called Russian Meddling when he was told about it by the FBI before the Election? Because he thought Crooked Hillary was going to win, and he didn't want to upset the apple cart! He was in charge, not me, and did nothing.

◯ 43.6K　　　↱↳ 32.6K　　　♡ 105.5K　　　↥

Donald J. Trump ✔ @realDonaldTrump · May 29, 2018   ○○○
Democrats mistakenly tweet 2014 pictures from Obama's term showing children from the Border in steel cages. They thought it was recent pictures in order to make us look bad, but backfires. Dems must agree to Wall and new Border Protection for good of country...Bipartisan Bill!

◯ 11.5K　　　↱↳ 24.7K　　　♡ 86.6K　　　↥

Donald J. Trump ✔ @realDonaldTrump · May 30, 2018   ○○○
Great meeting with @KimKardashian today, talked about prison reform and sentencing.

◯ 42K　　　↱↳ 109.3K　　　♡ 135.6K　　　↥

Donald J. Trump ✔ @realDonaldTrump · Jun 1, 2018   ○○○
Why aren't they firing no talent Samantha Bee for the horrible language used on her low ratings show? A total double standard but that's O.K., we are Winning, and will be doing so for a long time to come!

◯ 50.6K　　　↱↳ 31.9K　　　♡ 117K　　　↥

Donald J. Trump ✔ @realDonaldTrump · Jun 2, 2018   ○○○
The United States must, at long last, be treated fairly on Trade. If we charge a country ZERO to sell their goods, and they charge us 25, 50 or even 100 percent to sell ours, it is UNFAIR and can no longer be tolerated. That is not Free or Fair Trade, it is Stupid Trade!

◯ 15K　　　↱↳ 27.4K　　　♡ 107K　　　↥

Donald J. Trump ✓ @realDonaldTrump · Jun 4, 2018   ○○○

This is my 500th. Day in Office and we have accomplished a lot - many
believe more than any President in his first 500 days. Massive Tax &
Regulation Cuts, Military & Vets, Lower Crime & Illegal Immigration, Stronger
Borders, Judgeships, Best Economy & Jobs EVER, and much more...

💬 28.4K   ⟲ 26.3K   ♡ 109.3K   ↑

Donald J. Trump ✓ @realDonaldTrump · Jun 4, 2018   ○○○

The Philadelphia Eagles Football Team was invited to the White House.
Unfortunately, only a small number of players decided to come, and we
canceled the event. Staying in the Locker Room for the playing of our
National Anthem is as disrespectful to our country as kneeling. Sorry!

💬 45.2K   ⟲ 30.4K   ♡ 98.6K   ↑

Donald J. Trump ✓ @realDonaldTrump · Jun 10, 2018   ○○○

Sorry, we cannot let our friends, or enemies, take advantage of us on Trade
anymore. We must put the American worker first!

💬 25.5K   ⟲ 29.3K   ♡ 128.1K   ↑

Donald J. Trump ✓ @realDonaldTrump · Jun 12, 2018   ○○○

I want to thank Chairman Kim for taking the first bold step toward a bright
new future for his people. Our unprecedented meeting – the first between
an American President and a leader of North Korea – proves that real change
is possible!

💬 7.9K   ⟲ 20.7K   ♡ 94.4K   ↑

Donald J. Trump ✓ @realDonaldTrump · Jun 12, 2018   ○○○

The World has taken a big step back from potential Nuclear catastrophe! No
more rocket launches, nuclear testing or research! The hostages are back
home with their families. Thank you to Chairman Kim, our day together was
historic!

💬 14.3K   ⟲ 28.4K   ♡ 129.3K

Donald J. Trump ✔ @realDonaldTrump · Jun 13, 2018   ○○○

Robert De Niro, a very Low IQ individual, has received too many shots to the head by real boxers in movies. I watched him last night and truly believe he may be "punch-drunk." I guess he doesn't...

💬 11.2K   ⟲ 19.2K   ♡ 82.4K   ⬆️

Donald J. Trump ✔ @realDonaldTrump · Jun 13, 2018   ○○○

...realize the economy is the best it's ever been with employment being at an all time high, and many companies pouring back into our country. Wake up Punchy!

💬 4.8K   ⟲ 11.3K   ♡ 61.9K   ⬆️

Donald J. Trump ✔ @realDonaldTrump · Jun 13, 2018   ○○○

Before taking office people were assuming that we were going to War with North Korea. President Obama said that North Korea was our biggest and most dangerous problem. No longer - sleep well tonight!

💬 20.9K   ⟲ 29.6K   ♡ 122.4K   ⬆️

Donald J. Trump ✔ @realDonaldTrump · Jun 15, 2018   ○○○

I've had to beat 17 very talented people including the Bush Dynasty, then I had to beat the Clinton Dynasty, and now I have to beat a phony Witch Hunt and all of the dishonest people covered in the IG Report...and never forget the Fake News Media. It never ends!

💬 45.3K   ⟲ 35.7K   ♡ 129.1K   ⬆️

Donald J. Trump ✔ @realDonaldTrump · Jun 16, 2018   ○○○

My supporters are the smartest, strongest, most hard working and most loyal that we have seen in our countries history. It is a beautiful thing to watch as we win elections and gather support from all over the country. As we get stronger, so does our country. Best numbers ever!

💬 58.2K   ⟲ 44.3K   ♡ 156.2K   ⬆️

Donald J. Trump ✔ @realDonaldTrump · Jun 18, 2018   ○○○

We don't want what is happening with immigration in Europe to happen with us!

💬 22K   ⟲ 28.7K   ♡ 104.1K   ⬆️

Donald J. Trump ✔ @realDonaldTrump · Jun 18, 2018   ○○○

The people of Germany are turning against their leadership as migration is rocking the already tenuous Berlin coalition. Crime in Germany is way up. Big mistake made all over Europe in allowing millions of people in who have so strongly and violently changed their culture!

💬 33.9K   ⟲ 35.8K   ♡ 96.4K   ⬆️

Donald J. Trump ✔ @realDonaldTrump · Jun 19, 2018

If you don't have Borders, you don't have a Country!

💬 24K   ↻ 39.7K   ♡ 144.7K   ↑

Donald J. Trump ✔ @realDonaldTrump · Jun 21, 2018

"I REALLY DON'T CARE, DO U?" written on the back of Melania's jacket, refers to the Fake News Media. Melania has learned how dishonest they are, and she truly no longer cares!

💬 65.8K   ↻ 48.8K   ♡ 132.3K   ↑

Donald J. Trump ✔ @realDonaldTrump · Jun 21, 2018

We have to maintain strong borders or we will no longer have a country that we can be proud of – and if we show any weakness, millions of people will journey into our country.

💬 30.4K   ↻ 29.6K   ♡ 121K   ↑

Donald J. Trump ✔ @realDonaldTrump · Jun 23, 2018

It's very sad that Nancy Pelosi and her sidekick, Cryin' Chuck Schumer, want to protect illegal immigrants far more than the citizens of our country. The United States cannot stand for this. We wants safety and security at our borders!

💬 33.8K   ↻ 34.6K   ♡ 129.7K   ↑

Donald J. Trump ✔ @realDonaldTrump · Jun 24, 2018

.@jimmyfallon is now whimpering to all that he did the famous "hair show" with me (where he seriously messed up my hair), & that he would have now done it differently because it is said to have "humanized" me-he is taking heat. He called & said "monster ratings." Be a man Jimmy!

💬 28.9K   ↻ 22.2K   ♡ 79.2K   ↑

Donald J. Trump ✔ @realDonaldTrump · Jun 25, 2018

The Red Hen Restaurant should focus more on cleaning its filthy canopies, doors and windows (badly needs a paint job) rather than refusing to serve a fine person like Sarah Huckabee Sanders. I always had a rule, if a restaurant is dirty on the outside, it is dirty on the inside!

💬 70.6K   ↻ 46.7K   ♡ 116.4K   ↑

Donald J. Trump ✔ @realDonaldTrump · Jun 25, 2018

Congresswoman Maxine Waters, an extraordinarily low IQ person, has become, together with Nancy Pelosi, the Face of the Democrat Party. She has just called for harm to supporters, of which there are many, of the Make America Great Again movement. Be careful what you wish for Max!

💬 52.1K   ↻ 43.6K   ♡ 120.8K   ↑

Donald J. Trump ✔ @realDonaldTrump · Jun 26, 2018
SUPREME COURT UPHOLDS TRUMP TRAVEL BAN. Wow!

💬 30.6K   🔁 36K   ♡ 142.9K   ↑

Donald J. Trump ✔ @realDonaldTrump · Jul 1, 2018
The Liberal Left, also known as the Democrats, want to get rid of ICE, who do a fantastic job, and want Open Borders. Crime would be rampant and uncontrollable! Make America Great Again

💬 33.9K   🔁 27.2K   ♡ 110.8K   ↑

Donald J. Trump ✔ @realDonaldTrump · Jul 7, 2018
Twitter is getting rid of fake accounts at a record pace. Will that include the Failing New York Times and propaganda machine for Amazon, the Washington Post, who constantly quote anonymous sources that, in my opinion, don't exist - They will both be out of business in 7 years!

💬 44.2K   🔁 29.7K   ♡ 104.1K   ↑

Donald J. Trump ✔ @realDonaldTrump · Jul 8, 2018
Iranian Harassment of U.S. Warships:

2015: 22
2016: 36
2017: 14
2018: 0

Source: @USNavy

💬 14.4K   🔁 33.4K   ♡ 131.4K   ↑

Donald J. Trump ✔ @realDonaldTrump · Jul 8, 2018
They just didn't get it, but they do now!

💬 48.3K   🔁 145.1K   ♡ 303.3K   ↑

Donald J. Trump ✔ @realDonaldTrump · Jul 9, 2018   ○○○

Tonight, it was my honor and privilege to nominate Judge Brett Kavanaugh to the United States Supreme Court. #SCOTUS

💬 7.7K   🔁 13.6K   ♡ 67.5K   ⬆️

 Donald J. Trump ✔ @realDonaldTrump · Jul 10, 2018   ○○○

Just talked with Pfizer CEO and @SecAzar on our drug pricing blueprint. Pfizer is rolling back price hikes, so American patients don't pay more. We applaud Pfizer for this decision and hope other companies do the same. Great news for the American people!

💬 11.8K   🔁 22.4K   ♡ 90.5K   ⬆️

 Donald J. Trump ✔ @realDonaldTrump · Jul 14, 2018   ○○○

The Stock Market hit 25,000 yesterday. Jobs are at an all time record - and that is before we fix some of the worst trade deals and conditions ever seen by any government. It is all happening!

💬 8.5K   🔁 20.3K   ♡ 94.1K   ⬆️

 Donald J. Trump ✔ @realDonaldTrump · Jul 18, 2018   ○○○

Some people HATE the fact that I got along well with President Putin of Russia. They would rather go to war than see this. It's called Trump Derangement Syndrome!

💬 49.8K   🔁 32.4K   ♡ 107.3K   ⬆️

 Donald J. Trump ✔ @realDonaldTrump · Jul 20, 2018   ○○○

I got severely criticized by the Fake News Media for being too nice to President Putin. In the Old Days they would call it Diplomacy. If I was loud & vicious, I would have been criticized for being too tough. Remember when they said I was too tough with Chairman Kim? Hypocrites!

💬 46.7K   🔁 33.8K   ♡ 126.9K   ⬆️

Donald J. Trump ✓ @realDonaldTrump · Jul 22, 2018   ⦁⦁⦁

To Iranian President Rouhani: NEVER, EVER THREATEN THE UNITED STATES AGAIN OR YOU WILL SUFFER CONSEQUENCES THE LIKES OF WHICH FEW THROUGHOUT HISTORY HAVE EVER SUFFERED BEFORE. WE ARE NO LONGER A COUNTRY THAT WILL STAND FOR YOUR DEMENTED WORDS OF VIOLENCE & DEATH. BE CAUTIOUS!

💬 110.7K   ↻ 186.9K   ♡ 298.7K   ⬆

Donald J. Trump ✓ @realDonaldTrump · Jul 24, 2018   ⦁⦁⦁

MAKE AMERICA GREAT AGAIN!

💬 26K   ↻ 29.1K   ♡ 111.9K   ⬆

Donald J. Trump ✓ @realDonaldTrump · Jul 24, 2018   ⦁⦁⦁

The European Union is coming to Washington tomorrow to negotiate a deal on Trade. I have an idea for them. Both the U.S. and the E.U. drop all Tariffs, Barriers and Subsidies! That would finally be called Free Market and Fair Trade! Hope they do it, we are ready - but they won't!

💬 14.8K   ↻ 28.8K   ♡ 101.9K   ⬆

Donald J. Trump ✓ @realDonaldTrump · Jul 26, 2018   ⦁⦁⦁

Twitter "SHADOW BANNING" prominent Republicans. Not good. We will look into this discriminatory and illegal practice at once! Many complaints.

💬 35K   ↻ 49.5K   ♡ 132.8K   ⬆

Donald J. Trump ✓ @realDonaldTrump · Jul 29, 2018   ⦁⦁⦁

Wow, highest Poll Numbers in the history of the Republican Party. That includes Honest Abe Lincoln and Ronald Reagan. There must be something wrong, please recheck that poll!

💬 19.4K   ↻ 20.2K   ♡ 85.4K   ⬆

Donald J. Trump ✓ @realDonaldTrump · Jul 29, 2018   ⦁⦁⦁

I would be willing to "shut down" government if the Democrats do not give us the votes for Border Security, which includes the Wall! Must get rid of Lottery, Catch & Release etc. and finally go to system of Immigration based on MERIT! We need great people coming into our Country!

💬 52.1K   ↻ 36.4K   ♡ 112.8K   ⬆

Donald J. Trump ✓ @realDonaldTrump · Aug 2, 2018   ⦁⦁⦁

Thank you to Chairman Kim Jong Un for keeping your word & starting the process of sending home the remains of our great and beloved missing fallen! I am not at all surprised that you took this kind action. Also, thank you for your nice letter - I look forward to seeing you soon!

💬 22.1K   ↻ 24.7K   ♡ 109.7K   ⬆

Donald J. Trump ✔ @realDonaldTrump · Aug 2, 2018   ○○○

They asked my daughter Ivanka whether or not the media is the enemy of the people. She correctly said no. It is the FAKE NEWS, which is a large percentage of the media, that is the enemy of the people!

💬 37.6K   ⇄ 31.9K   ♡ 122.2K   ⬆

Donald J. Trump ✔ @realDonaldTrump · Aug 3, 2018   ○○○

NASA, which is making a BIG comeback under the Trump Administration, has just named 9 astronauts for Boeing and Spacex space flights. We have the greatest facilities in the world and we are now letting the private sector pay to use them. Exciting things happening. Space Force!

💬 9.5K   ⇄ 15.4K   ♡ 68K   ⬆

Donald J. Trump ✔ @realDonaldTrump · Aug 3, 2018   ○○○

Lebron James was just interviewed by the dumbest man on television, Don Lemon. He made Lebron look smart, which isn't easy to do. I like Mike!

💬 120.7K   ⇄ 135.7K   ♡ 151.7K   ⬆

Donald J. Trump ✔ @realDonaldTrump · Aug 7, 2018   ○○○

The Iran sanctions have officially been cast. These are the most biting sanctions ever imposed, and in November they ratchet up to yet another level. Anyone doing business with Iran will NOT be doing business with the United States. I am asking for WORLD PEACE, nothing less!

💬 25.3K   ⇄ 33.8K   ♡ 115.3K   ⬆

Donald J. Trump ✔ @realDonaldTrump · Aug 8, 2018   ○○○

The Republicans have now won 8 out of 9 House Seats, yet if you listen to the Fake News Media you would think we are being clobbered. Why can't they play it straight, so unfair to the Republican Party and in particular, your favorite President!

💬 24K   ⇄ 31.6K   ♡ 128.2K   ⬆

Donald J. Trump ✔ @realDonaldTrump · Aug 9, 2018   ○○○

Space Force all the way!

💬 43.2K   ⇄ 43.1K   ♡ 120.9K   ⬆

Donald J. Trump ✔ @realDonaldTrump · Aug 10, 2018   ○○○

Democrats, please do not distance yourselves from Nancy Pelosi. She is a wonderful person whose ideas & policies may be bad, but who should definitely be given a 4th chance. She is trying very hard & has every right to take down the Democrat Party if she has veered too far left!

💬 22.3K   ⇄ 30.7K   ♡ 118K   ⬆

Donald J. Trump ✔ @realDonaldTrump · Aug 11, 2018   ooo
The riots in Charlottesville a year ago resulted in senseless death and division. We must come together as a nation. I condemn all types of racism and acts of violence. Peace to ALL Americans!

💬 32.2K   ⟲ 32.3K   ♡ 114.2K   ⬆

Donald J. Trump ✔ @realDonaldTrump · Aug 11, 2018   ooo
I am proud to have fought for and secured the LOWEST African American and Hispanic unemployment rates in history. Now I'm pushing for prison reform to give people who have paid their debt to society a second chance. I will never stop fighting for ALL Americans!

💬 26K   ⟲ 32.4K   ♡ 128.1K   ⬆

Donald J. Trump ✔ @realDonaldTrump · Aug 13, 2018   ooo
While I know it's "not presidential" to take on a lowlife like Omarosa, and while I would rather not be doing so, this is a modern day form of communication and I know the Fake News Media will be working overtime to make even Wacky Omarosa look legitimate as possible. Sorry!

💬 34.4K   ⟲ 23K   ♡ 89.8K   ⬆

Donald J. Trump ✔ @realDonaldTrump · Aug 14, 2018   ooo
When you give a crazed, crying lowlife a break, and give her a job at the White House, I guess it just didn't work out. Good work by General Kelly for quickly firing that dog!

💬 63K   ⟲ 42.9K   ♡ 75.8K   ⬆

Donald J. Trump ✔ @realDonaldTrump · Aug 16, 2018   ooo
There is nothing that I would want more for our Country than true FREEDOM OF THE PRESS. The fact is that the Press is FREE to write and say anything it wants, but much of what it says is FAKE NEWS, pushing a political agenda or just plain trying to hurt people. HONESTY WINS!

💬 44.7K   ⟲ 34.5K   ♡ 112.6K   ⬆

Donald J. Trump ✔ @realDonaldTrump · Aug 16, 2018   ooo
How can "Senator" Richard Blumenthal, who went around for twenty years as a Connecticut politician bragging that he was a great Marine war hero in Vietnam (then got caught and sobbingly admitted he was neither a Marine nor ever in Vietnam), pass judgement on anyone? Loser!

💬 25.9K   ⟲ 26.9K   ♡ 91.4K   ⬆

Donald J. Trump ✔ @realDonaldTrump · Aug 22, 2018   ooo
If anyone is looking for a good lawyer, I would strongly suggest that you don't retain the services of Michael Cohen!

💬 67.7K   ⟲ 58.6K   ♡ 128.3K   ⬆

Donald J. Trump ✔ @realDonaldTrump · Aug 25, 2018

Stock Market hit all time high on Friday. Congratulations U.S.A.!

💬 17.6K   🔁 23.7K   ♡ 114.9K   ⬆️

Donald J. Trump ✔ @realDonaldTrump · Aug 25, 2018

My deepest sympathies and respect go out to the family of Senator John McCain. Our hearts and prayers are with you!

💬 80.5K   🔁 43.1K   ♡ 190.3K   ⬆️

Donald J. Trump ✔ @realDonaldTrump · Aug 26, 2018

Over 90% approval rating for your all time favorite (I hope) President within the Republican Party and 52% overall. This despite all of the made up stories by the Fake News Media trying endlessly to make me look as bad and evil as possible. Look at the real villains please!

💬 80.9K   🔁 44.6K   ♡ 152.1K   ⬆️

Donald J. Trump ✔ @realDonaldTrump · Aug 28, 2018

NASDAQ has just gone above 8000 for the first time in history!

💬 14.2K   🔁 24.4K   ♡ 101.1K   ⬆️

Donald J. Trump ✔ @realDonaldTrump · Aug 29, 2018

When you see "anonymous source," stop reading the story, it is fiction!

💬 34.8K   🔁 37.3K   ♡ 124.3K   ⬆️

Donald J. Trump ✔ @realDonaldTrump · Aug 30, 2018

I just cannot state strongly enough how totally dishonest much of the Media is. Truth doesn't matter to them, they only have their hatred & agenda. This includes fake books, which come out about me all the time, always anonymous sources, and are pure fiction. Enemy of the People!

💬 49.4K   🔁 32K   ♡ 105.6K   ⬆️

Donald J. Trump ✔ @realDonaldTrump · Sep 1, 2018

There is no political necessity to keep Canada in the new NAFTA deal. If we don't make a fair deal for the U.S. after decades of abuse, Canada will be out. Congress should not interfere w/ these negotiations or I will simply terminate NAFTA entirely & we will be far better off...

💬 26.3K   🔁 24.2K   ♡ 87.4K   ⬆️

Donald J. Trump ✔ @realDonaldTrump · Sep 1, 2018

MAKE AMERICA GREAT AGAIN!

💬 63.9K   🔁 42.2K   ♡ 148.8K   ⬆️

Donald J. Trump ✔ @realDonaldTrump · Sep 4, 2018 ⁰ᵒᵒ
The Brett Kavanaugh hearings for the future Justice of the Supreme Court are truly a display of how mean, angry, and despicable the other side is. They will say anything, and are only....

💬 12.7K   🔁 18.6K   ♡ 75.5K   ↑

Donald J. Trump ✔ @realDonaldTrump · Sep 4, 2018 ⁰ᵒᵒ
....looking to inflict pain and embarrassment to one of the most highly renowned jurists to ever appear before Congress. So sad to see!

💬 9K   🔁 12.8K   ♡ 55.6K   ↑

Donald J. Trump ✔ @realDonaldTrump · Sep 4, 2018 ⁰ᵒᵒ
Sleepy Eyes Chuck Todd of Fake NBC News said it's time for the Press to stop complaining and to start fighting back. Actually Chuck, they've been doing that from the day I announced for President. They've gone all out, and I WON, and now they're going CRAZY!

💬 18K   🔁 22.7K   ♡ 89.1K   ↑

Donald J. Trump ✔ @realDonaldTrump · Sep 5, 2018 ⁰ᵒᵒ
I'm draining the Swamp, and the Swamp is trying to fight back. Don't worry, we will win!

💬 53.9K   🔁 55.7K   ♡ 176.1K   ↑

Donald J. Trump ✔ @realDonaldTrump · Sep 7, 2018 ⁰ᵒᵒ
What was Nike thinking?

💬 48.8K   🔁 38.4K   ♡ 127.2K   ↑

Donald J. Trump ✔ @realDonaldTrump · Sep 9, 2018 ⁰ᵒᵒ
If the U.S. sells a car into China, there is a tax of 25%. If China sells a car into the U.S., there is a tax of 2%. Does anybody think that is FAIR? The days of the U.S. being ripped-off by other nations is OVER!

💬 15.3K   🔁 28.8K   ♡ 113.2K   ↑

Donald J. Trump ✔ @realDonaldTrump · Sep 10, 2018 ⁰ᵒᵒ
"President Trump would need a magic wand to get to 4% GDP," stated President Obama. I guess I have a magic wand, 4.2%, and we will do MUCH better than this! We have just begun.

💬 27.7K   🔁 37.6K   ♡ 128.9K   ↑

Donald J. Trump ✔ @realDonaldTrump · Sep 21, 2018 ⁰ᵒᵒ
Judge Brett Kavanaugh is a fine man, with an impeccable reputation, who is under assault by radical left wing politicians who don't want to know the answers, they just want to destroy and delay. Facts don't matter. I go through this with them every single day in D.C.

💬 26.2K   🔁 28.1K   ♡ 96.4K   ↑

Donald J. Trump ✔ @realDonaldTrump · Sep 26, 2018

Jobless Claims fell to their lowest level in 49 years!

💬 12.3K   🔁 17.9K   ♡ 82.2K   ⬆️

Donald J. Trump ✔ @realDonaldTrump · Sep 26, 2018

Avenatti is a third rate lawyer who is good at making false accusations, like he did on me and like he is now doing on Judge Brett Kavanaugh. He is just looking for attention and doesn't want people to look at his past record and relationships - a total low-life!

💬 51.1K   🔁 35.4K   ♡ 118K   ⬆️

Donald J. Trump ✔ @realDonaldTrump · Sep 27, 2018

Judge Kavanaugh showed America exactly why I nominated him. His testimony was powerful, honest, and riveting. Democrats' search and destroy strategy is disgraceful and this process has been a total sham and effort to delay, obstruct, and resist. The Senate must vote!

💬 89.1K   🔁 82.9K   ♡ 276.1K   ⬆️

Donald J. Trump ✔ @realDonaldTrump · Sep 29, 2018

Senator Richard Blumenthal must talk about his fraudulent service in Vietnam, where for 12 years he told the people of Connecticut, as their Attorney General, that he was a great Marine War Hero. Talked about his many battles of near death, but was never in Vietnam. Total Phony!

💬 33.2K   🔁 43K   ♡ 120.8K   ⬆️

Donald J. Trump ✔ @realDonaldTrump · Oct 1, 2018

Late last night, our deadline, we reached a wonderful new Trade Deal with Canada, to be added into the deal already reached with Mexico. The new name will be The United States Mexico Canada Agreement, or USMCA. It is a great deal for all three countries, solves the many......

💬 11.3K   🔁 26.1K   ♡ 111K   ⬆️

Donald J. Trump ✔ @realDonaldTrump · Oct 1, 2018

....deficiencies and mistakes in NAFTA, greatly opens markets to our Farmers and Manufacturers, reduces Trade Barriers to the U.S. and will bring all three Great Nations together in competition with the rest of the world. The USMCA is a historic transaction!

💬 5.4K   🔁 15.2K   ♡ 66.7K   ⬆️

Donald J. Trump ✔ @realDonaldTrump · Oct 2, 2018

THE ONLY REASON TO VOTE FOR A DEMOCRAT IS IF YOU'RE TIRED OF WINNING!

💬 33K   🔁 43.1K   ♡ 142.3K   ⬆️

Donald J. Trump ✔ @realDonaldTrump · Oct 3, 2018

The Stock Market just reached an All-Time High during my Administration for the 102nd Time, a presidential record, by far, for less than two years. So much potential as Trade and Military Deals are completed.

💬 8.7K   🔁 17.8K   ♡ 77.9K   ↑

Donald J. Trump ✔ @realDonaldTrump · Oct 4, 2018

This is now the 7th. time the FBI has investigated Judge Kavanaugh. If we made it 100, it would still not be good enough for the Obstructionist Democrats.

💬 19.3K   🔁 26.2K   ♡ 102.5K   ↑

Donald J. Trump ✔ @realDonaldTrump · Oct 5, 2018

The very rude elevator screamers are paid professionals only looking to make Senators look bad. Don't fall for it! Also, look at all of the professionally made identical signs. Paid for by Soros and others. These are not signs made in the basement from love! #Troublemakers

💬 60.7K   🔁 57.2K   ♡ 149.2K   ↑

Donald J. Trump ✔ @realDonaldTrump · Oct 6, 2018

I applaud and congratulate the U.S. Senate for confirming our GREAT NOMINEE, Judge Brett Kavanaugh, to the United States Supreme Court. Later today, I will sign his Commission of Appointment, and he will be officially sworn in. Very exciting!

💬 33.4K   🔁 59.6K   ♡ 222.9K   ↑

Donald J. Trump ✔ @realDonaldTrump · Oct 6, 2018

You don't hand matches to an arsonist, and you don't give power to an angry left-wing mob. Democrats have become too EXTREME and TOO DANGEROUS to govern. Republicans believe in the rule of law - not the rule of the mob. VOTE REPUBLICAN!

💬 57.2K   🔁 65.8K   ♡ 193.4K   ↑

Donald J. Trump ✔ @realDonaldTrump · Oct 16, 2018

Pocahontas (the bad version), sometimes referred to as Elizabeth Warren, is getting slammed. She took a bogus DNA test and it showed that she may be 1/1024, far less than the average American. Now Cherokee Nation denies her, "DNA test is useless." Even they don't want her. Phony!

💬 21.3K   🔁 25.8K   ♡ 102.6K   ↑

Donald J. Trump ✔ @realDonaldTrump · Oct 16, 2018

Anybody entering the United States illegally will be arrested and detained, prior to being sent back to their country!

💬 18.5K   🔁 38.3K   ♡ 144.5K   ↑

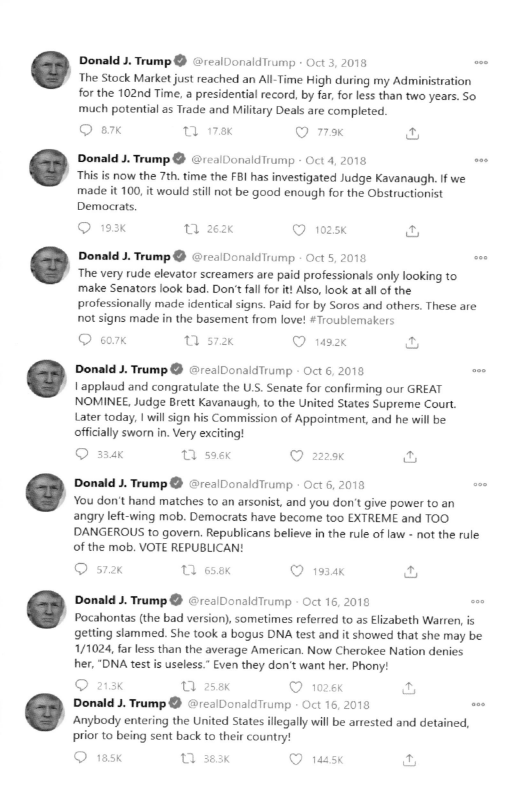

Donald J. Trump ✓ @realDonaldTrump · Oct 19, 2018

When referring to the USA, I will always capitalize the word Country!

💬 26.5K   ↻ 21.8K   ♡ 91.8K   ↑

Donald J. Trump ✓ @realDonaldTrump · Oct 21, 2018

Facebook has just stated that they are setting up a system to "purge" themselves of Fake News. Does that mean CNN will finally be put out of business?

💬 32.4K   ↻ 42.2K   ♡ 155.5K   ↑

Donald J. Trump ✓ @realDonaldTrump · Oct 22, 2018

Sadly, it looks like Mexico's Police and Military are unable to stop the Caravan heading to the Southern Border of the United States. Criminals and unknown Middle Easterners are mixed in. I have alerted Border Patrol and Military that this is a National Emergy. Must change laws!

💬 38.1K   ↻ 40.3K   ♡ 120.7K   ↑

Donald J. Trump ✓ @realDonaldTrump · Oct 22, 2018

Guatemala, Honduras and El Salvador were not able to do the job of stopping people from leaving their country and coming illegally to the U.S. We will now begin cutting off, or substantially reducing, the massive foreign aid routinely given to them.

💬 24.8K   ↻ 36.6K   ♡ 119.5K   ↑

Donald J. Trump ✓ @realDonaldTrump · Oct 25, 2018

A very big part of the Anger we see today in our society is caused by the purposely false and inaccurate reporting of the Mainstream Media that I refer to as Fake News. It has gotten so bad and hateful that it is beyond description. Mainstream Media must clean up its act, FAST!

💬 81.4K   ↻ 56K   ♡ 153.3K   ↑

Donald J. Trump ✓ @realDonaldTrump · Oct 25, 2018

To those in the Caravan, turnaround, we are not letting people into the United States illegally. Go back to your Country and if you want, apply for citizenship like millions of others are doing!

💬 24.3K   ↻ 41.3K   ♡ 132.2K   ↑

Donald J. Trump ✓ @realDonaldTrump · Oct 27, 2018

All of America is in mourning over the mass murder of Jewish Americans at the Tree of Life Synagogue in Pittsburgh. We pray for those who perished and their loved ones, and our hearts go out to the brave police officers who sustained serious injuries...

💬 9.6K   ↻ 20.6K   ♡ 88.6K   ↑

Donald J. Trump ✔ @realDonaldTrump · Oct 27, 2018

...This evil Anti-Semitic attack is an assault on humanity. It will take all of us working together to extract the poison of Anti-Semitism from our world. We must unite to conquer hate.

💬 18.2K　　🔁 18.9K　　♡ 73.5K　　⬆️

Donald J. Trump ✔ @realDonaldTrump · Nov 3, 2018

A vicious accuser of Justice Kavanaugh has just admitted that she was lying, her story was totally made up, or FAKE! Can you imagine if he didn't become a Justice of the Supreme Court because of her disgusting False Statements. What about the others? Where are the Dems on this?

💬 19.8K　　🔁 41.9K　　♡ 129.5K　　⬆️

Donald J. Trump ✔ @realDonaldTrump · Nov 6, 2018

Tremendous success tonight. Thank you to all!

💬 42.8K　　🔁 51.6K　　♡ 216.4K　　⬆️

Donald J. Trump ✔ @realDonaldTrump · Nov 9, 2018

You mean they are just now finding votes in Florida and Georgia – but the Election was on Tuesday? Let's blame the Russians and demand an immediate apology from President Putin!

💬 22.4K　　🔁 38.6K　　♡ 127.2K　　⬆️

Donald J. Trump ✔ @realDonaldTrump · Nov 10, 2018

There is no reason for these massive, deadly and costly forest fires in California except that forest management is so poor. Billions of dollars are given each year, with so many lives lost, all because of gross mismanagement of the forests. Remedy now, or no more Fed payments!

💬 96.8K　　🔁 74.3K　　♡ 107.5K　　⬆️

Donald J. Trump ✔ @realDonaldTrump · Nov 13, 2018

Emmanuel Macron suggests building its own army to protect Europe against the U.S., China and Russia. But it was Germany in World Wars One & Two - How did that work out for France? They were starting to learn German in Paris before the U.S. came along. Pay for NATO or not!

💬 31.2K　　🔁 42.8K　　♡ 104.8K　　⬆️

Donald J. Trump ✔ @realDonaldTrump · Nov 18, 2018

So funny to see little Adam Schitt (D-CA) talking about the fact that Acting Attorney General Matt Whitaker was not approved by the Senate, but not mentioning the fact that Bob Mueller (who is highly conflicted) was not approved by the Senate!

💬 66.3K　　🔁 44.6K　　♡ 112.5K　　⬆️

Donald J. Trump ✔ @realDonaldTrump · Nov 18, 2018 ⚬⚬⚬

Catch and Release is an obsolete term. It is now Catch and Detain. Illegal Immigrants trying to come into the U.S.A., often proudly flying the flag of their nation as they ask for U.S. Asylum, will be detained or turned away. Dems must approve Border Security & Wall NOW!

💬 23.2K   ⟲ 34.6K   ♡ 127.7K   ⬆

Donald J. Trump ✔ @realDonaldTrump · Nov 19, 2018 ⚬⚬⚬

The Fake News is showing old footage of people climbing over our Ocean Area Fence. This is what it really looks like - no climbers anymore under our Administration!

💬 35K   ⟲ 47K   ♡ 148K   ⬆

Donald J. Trump ✔ @realDonaldTrump · Nov 20, 2018 ⚬⚬⚬

So-called comedian Michelle Wolf bombed so badly last year at the White House Correspondents' Dinner that this year, for the first time in decades, they will have an author instead of a comedian. Good first step in comeback of a dying evening and tradition! Maybe I will go?

💬 41.6K   ⟲ 23.1K   ♡ 104.1K   ⬆

Donald J. Trump ✔ @realDonaldTrump · Nov 20, 2018 ⚬⚬⚬

AMERICA FIRST!

💬 36K   ⟲ 39.8K   ♡ 155K   ⬆

Donald J. Trump ✔ @realDonaldTrump · Nov 21, 2018 ⚬⚬⚬

You just can't win with the Fake News Media. A big story today is that because I have pushed so hard and gotten Gasoline Prices so low, more people are driving and I have caused traffic jams throughout our Great Nation. Sorry everyone!

💬 48.6K   ⟲ 39.1K   ♡ 144.9K   ⬆

Donald J. Trump ✔ @realDonaldTrump · Nov 22, 2018

HAPPY THANKSGIVING TO ALL!

💬 23.6K　　🔁 30.5K　　♡ 174.2K

Donald J. Trump ✔ @realDonaldTrump · Nov 21, 2018

MAKE AMERICA GREAT AGAIN!

💬 38.1K　　🔁 39.5K　　♡ 166.5K

Donald J. Trump ✔ @realDonaldTrump · Nov 26, 2018

Mexico should move the flag waving Migrants, many of whom are stone cold criminals, back to their countries. Do it by plane, do it by bus, do it anyway you want, but they are NOT coming into the U.S.A. We will close the Border permanently if need be. Congress, fund the WALL!

💬 36.5K　　🔁 43.2K　　♡ 147.6K

Donald J. Trump ✔ @realDonaldTrump · Dec 1, 2018

President George H.W. Bush led a long, successful and beautiful life. Whenever I was with him I saw his absolute joy for life and true pride in his family. His accomplishments were great from beginning to end. He was a truly wonderful man and will be missed by all!

💬 23.3K　　🔁 30K　　♡ 191.1K

Donald J. Trump ✔ @realDonaldTrump · Dec 3, 2018

"I will never testify against Trump." This statement was recently made by Roger Stone, essentially stating that he will not be forced by a rogue and out of control prosecutor to make up lies and stories about "President Trump." Nice to know that some people still have "guts!"

💬 40.5K　　🔁 27.5K　　♡ 84.8K

Donald J. Trump ✔ @realDonaldTrump · Dec 5, 2018

Looking forward to being with the Bush family. This is not a funeral, this is a day of celebration for a great man who has led a long and distinguished life. He will be missed!

💬 17.2K　　🔁 16.8K　　♡ 110.1K

Donald J. Trump ✔ @realDonaldTrump · Dec 6, 2018

FAKE NEWS - THE ENEMY OF THE PEOPLE!

💬 47.8K　　🔁 41.5K　　♡ 123.7K

Donald J. Trump ✔ @realDonaldTrump · Dec 7, 2018

Mike Pompeo is doing a great job, I am very proud of him. His predecessor, Rex Tillerson, didn't have the mental capacity needed. He was dumb as a rock and I couldn't get rid of him fast enough. He was lazy as hell. Now it is a whole new ballgame, great spirit at State!

💬 69.9K   ⟳ 46.8K   ♡ 94.2K   ↑

Donald J. Trump ✔ @realDonaldTrump · Dec 8, 2018

The Paris Agreement isn't working out so well for Paris. Protests and riots all over France. People do not want to pay large sums of money, much to third world countries (that are questionably run), in order to maybe protect the environment. Chanting "We Want Trump!" Love France.

💬 37.6K   ⟳ 40.5K   ♡ 116.1K   ↑

Donald J. Trump ✔ @realDonaldTrump · Dec 8, 2018

AFTER TWO YEARS AND MILLIONS OF PAGES OF DOCUMENTS (and a cost of over $30,000,000), NO COLLUSION!

💬 48.2K   ⟳ 28K   ♡ 101.3K   ↑

Donald J. Trump ✔ @realDonaldTrump · Dec 8, 2018

Very sad day & night in Paris. Maybe it's time to end the ridiculous and extremely expensive Paris Agreement and return money back to the people in the form of lower taxes? The U.S. was way ahead of the curve on that and the only major country where emissions went down last year!

💬 23K   ⟳ 34.9K   ♡ 128.1K   ↑

Donald J. Trump ✔ @realDonaldTrump · Dec 9, 2018

Leakin' James Comey must have set a record for who lied the most to Congress in one day. His Friday testimony was so untruthful! This whole deal is a Rigged Fraud headed up by dishonest people who would do anything so that I could not become President. They are now exposed!

💬 44.9K   ⟳ 29.6K   ♡ 105.4K   ↑

Donald J. Trump ✔ @realDonaldTrump · Dec 9, 2018

The Trump Administration has accomplished more than any other U.S. Administration in its first two (not even) years of existence, & we are having a great time doing it! All of this despite the Fake News Media, which has gone totally out of its mind-truly the Enemy of the People!

💬 57.8K   ⟳ 32.5K   ♡ 120.9K   ↑

Donald J. Trump ✔ @realDonaldTrump · Dec 14, 2018

As I predicted all along, Obamacare has been struck down as an UNCONSTITUTIONAL disaster! Now Congress must pass a STRONG law that provides GREAT healthcare and protects pre-existing conditions. Mitch and Nancy, get it done!

💬 23.8K   ⟳ 29.2K   ♡ 113.4K   ↑

Donald J. Trump ✔ @realDonaldTrump · Dec 19, 2018

We have defeated ISIS in Syria, my only reason for being there during the Trump Presidency.

💬 32.7K   🔁 28.1K   ♡ 98.8K   ⬆️

Donald J. Trump ✔ @realDonaldTrump · Dec 21, 2018

The Democrats now own the shutdown!

💬 98.7K   🔁 36.1K   ♡ 109.5K   ⬆️

Donald J. Trump ✔ @realDonaldTrump · Dec 21, 2018

Wishing Supreme Court Justice Ruth Bader Ginsburg a full and speedy recovery!

💬 16.9K   🔁 15.4K   ♡ 98K   ⬆️

Donald J. Trump ✔ @realDonaldTrump · Dec 22, 2018

I won an election, said to be one of the greatest of all time, based on getting out of endless & costly foreign wars & also based on Strong Borders which will keep our Country safe. We fight for the borders of other countries, but we won't fight for the borders of our own!

💬 59.1K   🔁 38.9K   ♡ 149.9K   ⬆️

Donald J. Trump ✔ @realDonaldTrump · Dec 24, 2018

AMERICA IS RESPECTED AGAIN!

💬 62.7K   🔁 34.4K   ♡ 134K   ⬆️

Donald J. Trump ✔ @realDonaldTrump · Dec 24, 2018

The only problem our economy has is the Fed. They don't have a feel for the Market, they don't understand necessary Trade Wars or Strong Dollars or even Democrat Shutdowns over Borders. The Fed is like a powerful golfer who can't score because he has no touch - he can't putt!

💬 49.7K   🔁 33.4K   ♡ 105.8K   ⬆️

Donald J. Trump ✔ @realDonaldTrump · Dec 24, 2018

Saudi Arabia has now agreed to spend the necessary money needed to help rebuild Syria, instead of the United States. See? Isn't it nice when immensely wealthy countries help rebuild their neighbors rather than a Great Country, the U.S., that is 5000 miles away. Thanks to Saudi A!

💬 32.4K   🔁 37.7K   ♡ 134K   ⬆️

Donald J. Trump ✔ @realDonaldTrump · Dec 24, 2018

I am all alone (poor me) in the White House waiting for the Democrats to come back and make a deal on desperately needed Border Security. At some point the Democrats not wanting to make a deal will cost our Country more money than the Border Wall we are all talking about. Crazy!

💬 110.8K   🔁 51.2K   ♡ 155.4K   ⬆️

Donald J. Trump ✔ @realDonaldTrump · Dec 25, 2018   ᵒᵒᵒ
Merry Christmas!

💬 86.9K   ⇄ 80.6K   ♡ 442K   ⬆️

Donald J. Trump ✔ @realDonaldTrump · Dec 25, 2018   ᵒᵒᵒ
I hope everyone, even the Fake News Media, is having a great Christmas!
Our Country is doing very well. We are securing our Borders, making great
new Trade Deals, and bringing our Troops Back Home. We are finally putting
America First. MERRY CHRISTMAS! #MAGA

💬 66K   ⇄ 43.6K   ♡ 215.1K   ⬆️

Donald J. Trump ✔ @realDonaldTrump · Dec 27, 2018   ᵒᵒᵒ
Just returned from visiting our troops in Iraq and Germany. One thing is
certain, we have incredible people representing our Country - people that
know how to win!

💬 21.4K   ⇄ 26.1K   ♡ 147.4K   ⬆️

Donald J. Trump ✔ @realDonaldTrump · Dec 27, 2018   ᵒᵒᵒ
CNN & others within the Fake News Universe were going wild about my
signing MAGA hats for our military in Iraq and Germany. If these brave
young people ask me to sign their hat, I will sign. Can you imagine my saying
NO? We brought or gave NO hats as the Fake News first reported!

💬 39.9K   ⇄ 39.5K   ♡ 156.4K   ⬆️

Donald J. Trump ✔ @realDonaldTrump · Dec 29, 2018   ᵒᵒᵒ
For those that naively ask why didn't the Republicans get approval to build
the Wall over the last year, it is because IN THE SENATE WE NEED 10
DEMOCRAT VOTES, and they will gives us "NONE" for Border Security! Now
we have to do it the hard way, with a Shutdown. Too bad! @FoxNews

💬 56.5K   ⇄ 34.1K   ♡ 126.5K   ⬆️

Donald J. Trump ✔ @realDonaldTrump · Dec 30, 2018   ᵒᵒᵒ
President and Mrs. Obama built/has a ten foot Wall around their D.C.
mansion/compound. I agree, totally necessary for their safety and security.
The U.S. needs the same thing, slightly larger version!

💬 67K   ⇄ 61.8K   ♡ 208.9K   ⬆️

Donald J. Trump ✔ @realDonaldTrump · Jan 1, 2019   ᵒᵒᵒ
HAPPY NEW YEAR TO EVERYONE, INCLUDING THE HATERS AND THE FAKE
NEWS MEDIA! 2019 WILL BE A FANTASTIC YEAR FOR THOSE NOT
SUFFERING FROM TRUMP DERANGEMENT SYNDROME. JUST CALM DOWN
AND ENJOY THE RIDE, GREAT THINGS ARE HAPPENING FOR OUR COUNTRY!

💬 69.3K   ⇄ 76.2K   ♡ 222.4K   ⬆️

Donald J. Trump ✔ @realDonaldTrump · Jan 1, 2019   ⦁⦁⦁
Gas prices are low and expected to go down this year. This would be good!

🗨 16.3K   ↻ 29.4K   ♡ 176.7K   ⬆

Donald J. Trump ✔ @realDonaldTrump · Jan 2, 2019   ⦁⦁⦁
Here we go with Mitt Romney, but so fast! Question will be, is he a Flake? I
hope not. Would much prefer that Mitt focus on Border Security and so many
other things where he can be helpful. I won big, and he didn't. He should be
happy for all Republicans. Be a TEAM player & WIN!

🗨 43K   ↻ 35.3K   ♡ 150.7K   ⬆

Donald J. Trump ✔ @realDonaldTrump · Jan 2, 2019   ⦁⦁⦁
Sadly, there can be no REAL Border Security without the Wall!

🗨 44.9K   ↻ 29.4K   ♡ 133.1K   ⬆

Donald J. Trump ✔ @realDonaldTrump · Jan 3, 2019   ⦁⦁⦁

Warren
—1/2020 th—
@realDailyWire

🗨 42.8K   ↻ 57.6K   ♡ 171.7K   ⬆

Donald J. Trump ✔ @realDonaldTrump · Jan 4, 2019   ⦁⦁⦁
As I have stated many times, if the Democrats take over the House or Senate,
there will be disruption to the Financial Markets. We won the Senate, they
won the House. Things will settle down. They only want to impeach me
because they know they can't win in 2020, too much success!

🗨 38.7K   ↻ 33.1K   ♡ 144.4K   ⬆

Donald J. Trump ✔ @realDonaldTrump · Jan 4, 2019   ⦁⦁⦁
How do you impeach a president who has won perhaps the greatest election
of all time, done nothing wrong (no Collusion with Russia, it was the Dems
that Colluded), had the most successful first two years of any president, and
is the most popular Republican in party history 93%?

🗨 122.2K   ↻ 62.3K   ♡ 219.3K   ⬆

Donald J. Trump ✔ @realDonaldTrump · Jan 5, 2019   ○○○
Thank you to Kanye West for your nice words. Criminal Justice Reform is now law - passed in a very bipartisan way!

◯ 8K   ⟲ 18.4K   ♡ 101K   ⬆️

Donald J. Trump ✔ @realDonaldTrump · Jan 5, 2019   ○○○
The Democrats want Billions of Dollars for Foreign Aid, but they don't want to spend a small fraction of that number on properly securing our Border. Figure that one out!

◯ 26.6K   ⟲ 32.4K   ♡ 112.1K   ⬆️

Donald J. Trump ✔ @realDonaldTrump · Jan 5, 2019   ○○○

THE
WALL
IS
COMING

◯ 72.6K   ⟲ 105K   ♡ 216.5K   ⬆️

Donald J. Trump ✔ @realDonaldTrump · Jan 9, 2019   ○○○
Just left a meeting with Chuck and Nancy, a total waste of time. I asked what is going to happen in 30 days if I quickly open things up, are you going to approve Border Security which includes a Wall or Steel Barrier? Nancy said, NO. I said bye-bye, nothing else works!

◯ 110.6K   ⟲ 64K   ♡ 217.3K   ⬆️

Donald J. Trump ✔ @realDonaldTrump · Jan 10, 2019   ○○○
Cryin Chuck told his favorite lie when he used his standard sound bite that I "slammed the table & walked out of the room. He had a temper tantrum." Because I knew he would say that, and after Nancy said no to proper Border Security, I politely said bye-bye and left, no slamming!

◯ 41.1K   ⟲ 31.8K   ♡ 134.1K   ⬆️

Donald J. Trump ✔ @realDonaldTrump · Jan 10, 2019   ooo

MAKE AMERICA GREAT AGAIN!

💬 40.2K   ⟲ 40.4K   ♡ 171.3K   ⬆

 Donald J. Trump ✔ @realDonaldTrump · Jan 10, 2019   ooo

Dear Diary...

>  **Jim Acosta** ✔ @Acosta · Jan 10, 2019
>
> The steel slats don't run the entire length of the border in the McAllen area. We found one part where there is a chain link fence. Occasionally migrants come thru but residents say their community is quite safe.

💬 27.1K   ⟲ 44.7K   ♡ 150.5K   ⬆

 Donald J. Trump ✔ @realDonaldTrump · Jan 12, 2019   ooo

Lyin' James Comey, Andrew McCabe, Peter S and his lover, agent Lisa Page, & more, all disgraced and/or fired and caught in the act. These are just some of the losers that tried to do a number on your President. Part of the Witch Hunt. Remember the "insurance policy?" This is it!

💬 27.2K   ⟲ 25K   ♡ 94.1K   ⬆

Donald J. Trump ✔ @realDonaldTrump · Jan 13, 2019   ⚬⚬⚬

If Elizabeth Warren, often referred to by me as Pocahontas, did this commercial from Bighorn or Wounded Knee instead of her kitchen, with her husband dressed in full Indian garb, it would have been a smash!

Instagram/Elizabeth Warren

Hold on a sec, I'm going to get me a beer.

◯ 39.3K   ⇄ 25.8K   ♡ 82.9K   ⬆

Donald J. Trump ✔ @realDonaldTrump · Jan 13, 2019   ⚬⚬⚬

Best line in the Elizabeth Warren beer catastrophe is, to her husband, "Thank you for being here. I'm glad you're here" It's their house, he's supposed to be there!

◯ 27.4K   ⇄ 27.9K   ♡ 119.4K   ⬆

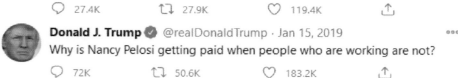

Donald J. Trump ✔ @realDonaldTrump · Jan 15, 2019   ⚬⚬⚬

Why is Nancy Pelosi getting paid when people who are working are not?

◯ 72K   ⇄ 50.6K   ♡ 183.2K   ⬆

Donald J. Trump ✔ @realDonaldTrump · Jan 17, 2019   ⚬⚬⚬

The Left has become totally unhinged. They no longer care what is Right for our Countrty!

◯ 66.9K   ⇄ 45.6K   ♡ 167.4K   ⬆

Donald J. Trump ✔ @realDonaldTrump · Jan 18, 2019   ○○○
AMERICA FIRST!

  💬 37.9K   ⟲ 33.9K   ♡ 135.5K   ⬆️

Donald J. Trump ✔ @realDonaldTrump · Jan 18, 2019   ○○○
Fake News is truly the ENEMY OF THE PEOPLE!

  💬 38.3K   ⟲ 42.7K   ♡ 146K   ⬆️

Donald J. Trump ✔ @realDonaldTrump · Jan 19, 2019   ○○○
.@newtgingrich just stated that there has been no president since Abraham
Lincoln who has been treated worse or more unfairly by the media than your
favorite President, me! At the same time there has been no president who
has accomplished more in his first two years in office!

  💬 44.9K   ⟲ 30.2K   ♡ 128.9K   ⬆️

Donald J. Trump ✔ @realDonaldTrump · Jan 20, 2019   ○○○
A truly great First Lady who doesn't get the credit she deserves!

Melania Trump ✔ @FLOTUS · Jan 20, 2019
🏳 US government account

It has been an unforgettable two years in the @WhiteHouse. I am
honored to serve this great nation! 🇺🇸

  💬 25.8K   ⟲ 28K   ♡ 142.7K   ⬆️

Donald J. Trump ✔ @realDonaldTrump · Jan 22, 2019   ○○○
Nick Sandmann and the students of Covington have become symbols of Fake
News and how evil it can be. They have captivated the attention of the world,
and I know they will use it for the good - maybe even to bring people
together. It started off unpleasant, but can end in a dream!

  💬 22.8K   ⟲ 34.2K   ♡ 138.1K   ⬆️

Donald J. Trump ✔ @realDonaldTrump · Jan 23, 2019   ⚬⚬⚬
BUILD A WALL & CRIME WILL FALL!

💬 73K   🔁 62.1K   ♡ 190.9K   ⬆

Donald J. Trump ✔ @realDonaldTrump · Jan 26, 2019   ⚬⚬⚬
Thank you to the Republican National Committee, (the RNC), who voted
UNANIMOUSLY yesterday to support me in the upcoming 2020 Election.
Considering that we have done more than any Administration in the first two
years, this should be easy. More great things now in the works!

💬 32.1K   🔁 36.4K   ♡ 179.1K   ⬆

Donald J. Trump ✔ @realDonaldTrump · Jan 28, 2019   ⚬⚬⚬
Numerous states introducing Bible Literacy classes, giving students the
option of studying the Bible. Starting to make a turn back? Great!

💬 57.1K   🔁 58.2K   ♡ 224.6K   ⬆

Donald J. Trump ✔ @realDonaldTrump · Jan 28, 2019   ⚬⚬⚬
In the beautiful Midwest, windchill temperatures are reaching minus 60
degrees, the coldest ever recorded. In coming days, expected to get even
colder. People can't last outside even for minutes. What the hell is going on
with Global Waming? Please come back fast, we need you!

💬 124.2K   🔁 123.5K   ♡ 182.8K   ⬆

Donald J. Trump ✔ @realDonaldTrump · Feb 2, 2019   ⚬⚬⚬
Democrat Governor Ralph Northam of Virginia just stated, "I believe that I
am not either of the people in that photo." This was 24 hours after
apologizing for appearing in the picture and after making the most horrible
statement on "super" late term abortion. Unforgivable!

💬 32.4K   🔁 31.8K   ♡ 131.8K   ⬆

Donald J. Trump ✔ @realDonaldTrump · Feb 9, 2019   ⚬⚬⚬
Today Elizabeth Warren, sometimes referred to by me as Pocahontas, joined
the race for President. Will she run as our first Native American presidential
candidate, or has she decided that after 32 years, this is not playing so well
anymore? See you on the campaign TRAIL, Liz!

💬 58.5K   🔁 58.6K   ♡ 167.8K   ⬆

Donald J. Trump ✔ @realDonaldTrump · Feb 9, 2019   ⚬⚬⚬
I think it is very important for the Democrats to press forward with their
Green New Deal. It would be great for the so-called "Carbon Footprint" to
permanently eliminate all Planes, Cars, Cows, Oil, Gas & the Military - even if
no other country would do the same. Brilliant!

💬 35.3K   🔁 39.7K   ♡ 151.4K   ⬆

Donald J. Trump ✔ @realDonaldTrump · Feb 10, 2019 ⚬⚬⚬

Well, it happened again. Amy Klobuchar announced that she is running for President, talking proudly of fighting global warming while standing in a virtual blizzard of snow, ice and freezing temperatures. Bad timing. By the end of her speech she looked like a Snowman(woman)!

💬 68.1K   ↻ 44.5K   ♡ 145.7K   ⬆️

Donald J. Trump ✔ @realDonaldTrump · Feb 11, 2019 ⚬⚬⚬

No president ever worked harder than me (cleaning up the mess I inherited)!

💬 62.2K   ↻ 38.9K   ♡ 167K   ⬆️

Donald J. Trump ✔ @realDonaldTrump · Feb 11, 2019 ⚬⚬⚬

The Democrats are so self righteous and ANGRY! Loosen up and have some fun. The Country is doing well!

💬 30K   ↻ 31.1K   ♡ 129.4K   ⬆️

Donald J. Trump ✔ @realDonaldTrump · Feb 16, 2019 ⚬⚬⚬

BUILDING THE WALL!

💬 50K   ↻ 66.7K   ♡ 258.8K   ⬆️

Donald J. Trump ✔ @realDonaldTrump · Feb 17, 2019 ⚬⚬⚬

THE RIGGED AND CORRUPT MEDIA IS THE ENEMY OF THE PEOPLE!

💬 67.3K   ↻ 56.2K   ♡ 176K   ⬆️

Donald J. Trump ✔ @realDonaldTrump · Feb 18, 2019 ⚬⚬⚬

I ask every member of the Maduro regime: End this nightmare of poverty, hunger and death. LET YOUR PEOPLE GO. Set your country free! Now is the time for all Venezuelan Patriots to act together, as one united people. Nothing could be better for the future of Venezuela!

💬 13.5K   ↻ 38.2K   ♡ 130.1K   ⬆️

Donald J. Trump ✔ @realDonaldTrump · Feb 20, 2019 ⚬⚬⚬

Crazy Bernie has just entered the race. I wish him well!

💬 22.4K   ↻ 28.2K   ♡ 142.4K   ⬆️

Donald J. Trump ✔ @realDonaldTrump · Feb 23, 2019 ⚬⚬⚬

God Bless the people of Venezuela!

💬 15.9K   ↻ 56.8K   ♡ 181.6K   ⬆️

Donald J. Trump ✔ @realDonaldTrump · Feb 24, 2019 ⚬⚬⚬

HOLD THE DATE! We will be having one of the biggest gatherings in the history of Washington, D.C., on July 4th. It will be called "A Salute To America" and will be held at the Lincoln Memorial. Major fireworks display, entertainment and an address by your favorite President, me!

💬 75.3K   ↻ 58.2K   ♡ 178.3K   ⬆️

Donald J. Trump ✔ @realDonaldTrump · Mar 5, 2019 ⚬⚬⚬

Republican Approval Rating just hit 93%. Sorry Haters! MAKE AMERICA GREAT AGAIN!

💬 35.6K ↻ 35.9K ♡ 136.5K ⬆

Donald J. Trump ✔ @realDonaldTrump · Mar 5, 2019 ⚬⚬⚬

"(Crooked) Hillary Clinton confirms she will not run in 2020, rules out a third bid for White House." Aw-shucks, does that mean I won't get to run against her again? She will be sorely missed!

💬 43.6K ↻ 32.8K ♡ 144.5K ⬆

Donald J. Trump ✔ @realDonaldTrump · Mar 6, 2019 ⚬⚬⚬

Democrats just blocked @FoxNews from holding a debate. Good, then I think I'll do the same thing with the Fake News Networks and the Radical Left Democrats in the General Election debates!

💬 47.9K ↻ 41.1K ♡ 155.8K ⬆

Donald J. Trump ✔ @realDonaldTrump · Mar 11, 2019 ⚬⚬⚬

Making Daylight Saving Time permanent is O.K. with me!

💬 22.3K ↻ 38.2K ♡ 170.4K ⬆

Donald J. Trump ✔ @realDonaldTrump · Mar 14, 2019 ⚬⚬⚬

I look forward to VETOING the just passed Democrat inspired Resolution which would OPEN BORDERS while increasing Crime, Drugs, and Trafficking in our Country. I thank all of the Strong Republicans who voted to support Border Security and our desperately needed WALL!

💬 41.2K ↻ 39K ♡ 149.1K ⬆

Donald J. Trump ✔ @realDonaldTrump · Mar 18, 2019 ⚬⚬⚬

While the press doesn't like writing about it, nor do I need them to, I donate my yearly Presidential salary of $400,000.00 to different agencies throughout the year, this to Homeland Security. If I didn't do it there would be hell to pay from the FAKE NEWS MEDIA!

💬 49.3K ↻ 47K ♡ 152.5K ⬆

Donald J. Trump ✔ @realDonaldTrump · Mar 22, 2019

3.1 GDP FOR THE YEAR, BEST NUMBER IN 14 YEARS!

💬 17.7K   🔁 31.3K   ♡ 145.5K   ↑

Donald J. Trump ✔ @realDonaldTrump · Mar 24, 2019

Good Morning, Have A Great Day!

💬 61.4K   🔁 73.8K   ♡ 402.2K   ↑

Donald J. Trump ✔ @realDonaldTrump · Mar 24, 2019

MAKE AMERICA GREAT AGAIN!

💬 42K   🔁 57.8K   ♡ 298.6K   ↑

Donald J. Trump ✔ @realDonaldTrump · Mar 24, 2019

No Collusion, No Obstruction, Complete and Total EXONERATION. KEEP AMERICA GREAT!

💬 87.3K   🔁 90.7K   ♡ 354.4K   ↑

Donald J. Trump ✔ @realDonaldTrump · Mar 25, 2019

"Breaking News: Mueller Report Finds No Trump-Russia Conspiracy." @MSNBC

💬 10.1K   🔁 17.1K   ♡ 90.6K   ↑

Donald J. Trump ✔ @realDonaldTrump · Mar 28, 2019

The Fake News Media is going Crazy! They are suffering a major "breakdown," have ZERO credibility or respect, & must be thinking about going legit. I have learned to live with Fake News, which has never been more corrupt than it is right now. Someday, I will tell you the secret!

💬 23.9K   🔁 33.6K   ♡ 137.4K   ↑

Donald J. Trump ✔ @realDonaldTrump · Mar 28, 2019

FBI & DOJ to review the outrageous Jussie Smollett case in Chicago. It is an embarrassment to our Nation!

💬 26.9K   🔁 31.9K   ♡ 117.3K   ↑

Donald J. Trump ✔ @realDonaldTrump · Mar 29, 2019

So funny that The New York Times & The Washington Post got a Pulitzer Prize for their coverage (100% NEGATIVE and FAKE!) of Collusion with Russia - And there was No Collusion! So, they were either duped or corrupt? In any event, their prizes should be taken away by the Committee!

💬 29.1K   🔁 31.8K   ♡ 126.9K   ↑

Donald J. Trump ✔ @realDonaldTrump · Apr 4, 2019

THE REPUBLICAN PARTY IS THE PARTY OF THE AMERICAN DREAM!

💬 32.2K   ↻ 29.7K   ♡ 131K   ⬆️

Donald J. Trump ✔ @realDonaldTrump · Apr 10, 2019

So, it has now been determined, by 18 people that truly hate President Trump, that there was No Collusion with Russia. In fact, it was an illegal investigation that should never have been allowed to start. I fought back hard against this Phony & Treasonous Hoax!

💬 33.7K   ↻ 32.7K   ♡ 139.3K   ⬆️

Donald J. Trump ✔ @realDonaldTrump · Apr 12, 2019

Due to the fact that Democrats are unwilling to change our very dangerous immigration laws, we are indeed, as reported, giving strong considerations to placing Illegal Immigrants in Sanctuary Cities only....

💬 44.2K   ↻ 41.9K   ♡ 147.4K   ⬆️

Donald J. Trump ✔ @realDonaldTrump · Apr 12, 2019

....The Radical Left always seems to have an Open Borders, Open Arms policy – so this should make them very happy!

💬 15.4K   ↻ 22.6K   ♡ 103.3K   ⬆️

Donald J. Trump ✔ @realDonaldTrump · Apr 13, 2019

Just out: The USA has the absolute legal right to have apprehended illegal immigrants transferred to Sanctuary Cities. We hereby demand that they be taken care of at the highest level, especially by the State of California, which is well known or its poor management & high taxes!

💬 37.2K   ↻ 42.3K   ♡ 146.7K   ⬆️

Donald J. Trump ✔ @realDonaldTrump · Apr 15, 2019

What do I know about branding, maybe nothing (but I did become President!), but if I were Boeing, I would FIX the Boeing 737 MAX, add some additional great features, & REBRAND the plane with a new name.
No product has suffered like this one. But again, what the hell do I know?

💬 37.8K   ↻ 25.5K   ♡ 109.7K   ⬆️

Donald J. Trump ✔ @realDonaldTrump · Apr 15, 2019

THEY SPIED ON MY CAMPAIGN (We will never forget)!

💬 24.9K   ↻ 32.5K   ♡ 123.5K   ⬆️

Donald J. Trump ✓ @realDonaldTrump · Apr 15, 2019 ⚬⚬⚬

Spoke to @TigerWoods to congratulate him on the great victory he had in yesterday's @TheMasters, & to inform him that because of his incredible Success & Comeback in Sports (Golf) and, more importantly, LIFE, I will be presenting him with the PRESIDENTIAL MEDAL OF FREEDOM!

◯ 16.9K   ⟲ 33.2K   ♡ 151.1K   ⬆

 Donald J. Trump ✓ @realDonaldTrump · Apr 18, 2019 ⚬⚬⚬

◯ 90.7K   ⟲ 137.7K   ♡ 346.9K   ⬆

 Donald J. Trump ✓ @realDonaldTrump · Apr 21, 2019 ⚬⚬⚬

Can you believe that I had to go through the worst and most corrupt political Witch Hunt in the history of the United States (No Collusion) when it was the "other side" that illegally created the diversionary & criminal event and even spied on my campaign? Disgraceful!

◯ 60.2K   ⟲ 39.5K   ♡ 162.1K   ⬆

 Donald J. Trump ✓ @realDonaldTrump · Apr 23, 2019 ⚬⚬⚬

You mean the Stock Market hit an all-time record high today and they're actually talking impeachment!? Will I ever be given credit for anything by the Fake News Media or Radical Liberal Dems? NO COLLUSION!

◯ 34.5K   ⟲ 31.9K   ♡ 130.1K   ⬆

 Donald J. Trump ✓ @realDonaldTrump · May 3, 2019 ⚬⚬⚬

I am continuing to monitor the censorship of AMERICAN CITIZENS on social media platforms. This is the United States of America — and we have what's known as FREEDOM OF SPEECH! We are monitoring and watching, closely!!

◯ 44.2K   ⟲ 55.8K   ♡ 174.6K   ⬆

Donald J. Trump ✔ @realDonaldTrump · May 4, 2019

How can it be possible that James Woods (and many others), a strong but responsible Conservative Voice, is banned from Twitter? Social Media & Fake News Media, together with their partner, the Democrat Party, have no idea the problems they are causing for themselves. VERY UNFAIR!

💬 30.1K   ↻ 42K   ♡ 140.2K   ⬆️

Donald J. Trump ✔ @realDonaldTrump · May 8, 2019

Big announcement today: Drug companies have to come clean about their prices in TV ads. Historic transparency for American patients is here. If drug companies are ashamed of those prices—lower them!

💬 11.9K   ↻ 26.7K   ♡ 118.5K   ⬆️

Donald J. Trump ✔ @realDonaldTrump · May 10, 2019

Build your products in the United States and there are NO TARIFFS!

💬 13.5K   ↻ 21.4K   ♡ 88.5K   ⬆️

Donald J. Trump ✔ @realDonaldTrump · May 10, 2019

Your all time favorite President got tired of waiting for China to help out and start buying from our FARMERS, the greatest anywhere in the World!

💬 27.7K   ↻ 21.5K   ♡ 102.1K   ⬆️

Donald J. Trump ✔ @realDonaldTrump · May 11, 2019

Such an easy way to avoid Tariffs? Make or produce your goods and products in the good old USA. It's very simple!

💬 28.7K   ↻ 27.9K   ♡ 118.3K   ⬆️

Donald J. Trump ✔ @realDonaldTrump · May 12, 2019

China is DREAMING that Sleepy Joe Biden, or any of the others, gets elected in 2020. They LOVE ripping off America!

💬 14K   ↻ 16.8K   ♡ 68.7K   ⬆️

Donald J. Trump ✔ @realDonaldTrump · May 13, 2019

Democrat Rep. Tlaib is being slammed for her horrible and highly insensitive statement on the Holocaust. She obviously has tremendous hatred of Israel and the Jewish people. Can you imagine what would happen if I ever said what she said, and says?

💬 24.4K   ↻ 27.1K   ♡ 94.2K   ⬆️

Donald J. Trump ✔ @realDonaldTrump · May 13, 2019

Under my Administration, we are restoring @NASA to greatness and we are going back to the Moon, then Mars. I am updating my budget to include an additional $1.6 billion so that we can return to Space in a BIG WAY!

💬 11.6K   ↻ 18.4K   ♡ 75.8K   ⬆️

Donald J. Trump ✔ @realDonaldTrump · May 17, 2019 ○○○

All people that are illegally coming into the United States now will be removed from our Country at a later date as we build up our removal forces and as the laws are changed. Please do not make yourselves too comfortable, you will be leaving soon!

💬 25.4K   🔁 45K   ♡ 152.4K   ⬆

Donald J. Trump ✔ @realDonaldTrump · May 17, 2019 ○○○

MAKE AMERICA GREAT AGAIN!

💬 25.2K   🔁 38.5K   ♡ 181.1K   ⬆

Donald J. Trump ✔ @realDonaldTrump · May 17, 2019 ○○○

My Campaign for President was conclusively spied on. Nothing like this has ever happened in American Politics. A really bad situation. TREASON means long jail sentences, and this was TREASON!

💬 46.1K   🔁 50.4K   ♡ 135.8K   ⬆

Donald J. Trump ✔ @realDonaldTrump · May 19, 2019 ○○○

If Iran wants to fight, that will be the official end of Iran. Never threaten the United States again!

💬 52.6K   🔁 88.6K   ♡ 206K   ⬆

Donald J. Trump ✔ @realDonaldTrump · May 22, 2019 ○○○

PRESIDENTIAL HARASSMENT!

💬 27K   🔁 27.4K   ♡ 96.9K   ⬆

Donald J. Trump ✔ @realDonaldTrump · May 23, 2019 ○○○

When is Twitter going to allow the very popular Conservative Voices that it has so viciously shut down, back into the OPEN? IT IS TIME!

💬 18.8K   🔁 34.3K   ♡ 125.1K   ⬆

Donald J. Trump ✔ @realDonaldTrump · May 25, 2019 ○○○

North Korea fired off some small weapons, which disturbed some of my people, and others, but not me. I have confidence that Chairman Kim will keep his promise to me, & also smiled when he called Swampman Joe Biden a low IQ individual, & worse. Perhaps that's sending me a signal?

💬 32.7K   🔁 23.9K   ♡ 88.2K   ⬆

Donald J. Trump ✔ @realDonaldTrump · May 28, 2019 ○○○

I was actually sticking up for Sleepy Joe Biden while on foreign soil. Kim Jong Un called him a "low IQ idiot," and many other things, whereas I related the quote of Chairman Kim as a much softer "low IQ individual." Who could possibly be upset with that?

💬 59.1K   🔁 30.3K   ♡ 110.4K   ⬆

Donald J. Trump ✓ @realDonaldTrump · May 29, 2019

How do you impeach a Republican President for a crime that was committed by the Democrats? WITCH-HUNT!

💬 49.9K   🔁 41.5K   ♡ 154.8K   ⬆️

Donald J. Trump ✓ @realDonaldTrump · Jun 3, 2019

....Kahn reminds me very much of our very dumb and incompetent Mayor of NYC, de Blasio, who has also done a terrible job - only half his height. In any event, I look forward to being a great friend to the United Kingdom, and am looking very much forward to my visit. Landing now!

💬 23K   🔁 29.6K   ♡ 127.9K   ⬆️

Donald J. Trump ✓ @realDonaldTrump · Jun 4, 2019

Washed up psycho @BetteMidler was forced to apologize for a statement she attributed to me that turned out to be totally fabricated by her in order to make "your great president" look really bad. She got caught, just like the Fake News Media gets caught. A sick scammer!

💬 46.3K   🔁 31.4K   ♡ 112.6K   ⬆️

Donald J. Trump ✓ @realDonaldTrump · Jun 7, 2019

I am pleased to inform you that The United States of America has reached a signed agreement with Mexico. The Tariffs scheduled to be implemented by the U.S. on Monday, against Mexico, are hereby indefinitely suspended. Mexico, in turn, has agreed to take strong measures to....

💬 29.3K   🔁 56.1K   ♡ 208.9K   ⬆️

Donald J. Trump ✓ @realDonaldTrump · Jun 7, 2019

....stem the tide of Migration through Mexico, and to our Southern Border. This is being done to greatly reduce, or eliminate, Illegal Immigration coming from Mexico and into the United States. Details of the agreement will be released shortly by the State Department. Thank you!

💬 18.5K   🔁 34K   ♡ 163K   ⬆️

Donald J. Trump ✓ @realDonaldTrump · Jun 8, 2019

MEXICO HAS AGREED TO IMMEDIATELY BEGIN BUYING LARGE QUANTITIES OF AGRICULTURAL PRODUCT FROM OUR GREAT PATRIOT FARMERS!

💬 25.5K   🔁 33.9K   ♡ 150.6K   ⬆️

Donald J. Trump ✓ @realDonaldTrump · Jun 9, 2019

I know it is not at all "Presidential" to hit back at the Corrupt Media, or people who work for the Corrupt Media, when they make false statements about me or the Trump Administration. Problem is, if you don't hit back, people believe the Fake News is true. So we'll hit back!

💬 39.5K   🔁 41K   ♡ 155K   ⬆️

Donald J. Trump ✔ @realDonaldTrump · Jun 9, 2019

Twitter should let the banned Conservative Voices back onto their platform, without restriction. It's called Freedom of Speech, remember. You are making a Giant Mistake!

💬 32.5K   🔁 50.2K   ♡ 153.8K   ⬆️

Donald J. Trump ✔ @realDonaldTrump · Jun 11, 2019

The United States has VERY LOW INFLATION, a beautiful thing!

💬 7.6K   🔁 14.9K   ♡ 77.1K   ⬆️

Donald J. Trump ✔ @realDonaldTrump · Jun 13, 2019

General Michael Flynn, the 33 year war hero who has served with distinction, has not retained a good lawyer, he has retained a GREAT LAWYER, Sidney Powell. Best Wishes and Good Luck to them both!

💬 10.4K   🔁 21.4K   ♡ 81.2K   ⬆️

Donald J. Trump ✔ @realDonaldTrump · Jun 13, 2019

After 3 1/2 years, our wonderful Sarah Huckabee Sanders will be leaving the White House at the end of the month and going home to the Great State of Arkansas....

💬 38.8K   🔁 28.1K   ♡ 127K   ⬆️

Donald J. Trump ✔ @realDonaldTrump · Jun 13, 2019

....She is a very special person with extraordinary talents, who has done an incredible job! I hope she decides to run for Governor of Arkansas - she would be fantastic. Sarah, thank you for a job well done!

💬 20.2K   🔁 20.7K   ♡ 123.3K   ⬆️

Donald J. Trump ✔ @realDonaldTrump · Jun 16, 2019

Happy Father's Day to all, including my worst and most vicious critics, of which there are fewer and fewer. This is a FANTASTIC time to be an American! KEEP AMERICA GREAT!

💬 33K   🔁 29.2K   ♡ 145.2K   ⬆️

Donald J. Trump ✔ @realDonaldTrump · Jun 16, 2019

Rep. Alexandria Ocasio-Cortez. "I think we have a very real risk of losing the Presidency to Donald Trump." I agree, and that is the only reason they play the impeach card, which cannot be legally used!

💬 20.9K   🔁 24.2K   ♡ 115.8K   ⬆️

Donald J. Trump ✔ @realDonaldTrump · Jun 20, 2019

Iran made a very big mistake!

💬 63.7K   🔁 71.2K   ♡ 213.6K   ⬆

 Donald J. Trump ✔ @realDonaldTrump · Jun 21, 2019

💬 70.9K   🔁 146.9K   ♡ 272.3K   ⬆

 Donald J. Trump ✔ @realDonaldTrump · Jun 22, 2019

When people come into our Country illegally, they will be DEPORTED!

💬 25.8K   🔁 38.1K   ♡ 172.9K   ⬆

 Donald J. Trump ✔ @realDonaldTrump · Jun 26, 2019

BORING!

💬 62.4K   🔁 99.8K   ♡ 289.2K   ⬆

Donald J. Trump ✔ @realDonaldTrump · Jun 27, 2019   ooo
All Democrats just raised their hands for giving millions of illegal aliens
unlimited healthcare. How about taking care of American Citizens first!? That's
the end of that race!

💬 46.7K   ⟲ 68.8K   ♡ 256.4K   ⬆

Donald J. Trump ✔ @realDonaldTrump · Jun 28, 2019   ooo
After some very important meetings, including my meeting with President Xi
of China, I will be leaving Japan for South Korea (with President Moon). While
there, if Chairman Kim of North Korea sees this, I would meet him at the
Border/DMZ just to shake his hand and say Hello(?)!

💬 33.9K   ⟲ 40.6K   ♡ 146.9K   ⬆

Donald J. Trump ✔ @realDonaldTrump · Jun 30, 2019   ooo
Leaving South Korea after a wonderful meeting with Chairman Kim Jong Un.
Stood on the soil of North Korea, an important statement for all, and a great
honor!

💬 37.3K   ⟲ 40.3K   ♡ 181.7K   ⬆

Donald J. Trump ✔ @realDonaldTrump · Jul 2, 2019   ooo

💬 13K   ⟲ 33.8K   ♡ 163.4K   ⬆

Donald J. Trump ✔ @realDonaldTrump · Jul 3, 2019   ooo
If Illegal Immigrants are unhappy with the conditions in the quickly built or
refitted detentions centers, just tell them not to come. All problems solved!

💬 52.4K   ⟲ 79.2K   ♡ 240.1K   ⬆

Donald J. Trump ✔ @realDonaldTrump · Jul 3, 2019   ooo
Mexico is doing a far better job than the Democrats on the Border. Thank you
Mexico!

💬 9.1K   ⟲ 21.5K   ♡ 103.5K   ⬆

Donald J. Trump ✔ @realDonaldTrump · Jul 3, 2019 ooo

Today's Stock Market is the highest in the history of our great Country! This is the 104th time since the Election of 2016 that we have reached a NEW HIGH. Congratulations USA!

💬 12.7K   ⟲ 22.6K   ♡ 113.4K   ⬆

Donald J. Trump ✔ @realDonaldTrump · Jul 4, 2019 ooo

Great news for the Republican Party as one of the dumbest & most disloyal men in Congress is "quitting" the Party. No Collusion, No Obstruction! Knew he couldn't get the nomination to run again in the Great State of Michigan. Already being challenged for his seat. A total loser!

💬 38K   ⟲ 25.2K   ♡ 98.4K   ⬆

Donald J. Trump ✔ @realDonaldTrump · Jul 7, 2019 ooo

Sleepy Joe Biden just admitted he worked with segregationists and separately, has already been very plain about the fact that he will be substantially raising everyone's taxes if he becomes president. Ridiculously, all Democrats want to substantially raise taxes!

💬 22.2K   ⟲ 20.7K   ♡ 84.8K   ⬆

Donald J. Trump ✔ @realDonaldTrump · Jul 7, 2019 ooo

Congratulations to the U.S. Women's Soccer Team on winning the World Cup! Great and exciting play. America is proud of you all!

💬 22.1K   ⟲ 30K   ♡ 236.1K   ⬆

Donald J. Trump ✔ @realDonaldTrump · Jul 13, 2019 ooo

94% Approval Rating in the Republican Party, an all time high. Ronald Reagan was 87%. Thank you!

💬 32.9K   ⟲ 36.8K   ♡ 177.5K   ⬆

Donald J. Trump ✔ @realDonaldTrump · Jul 14, 2019 ooo

So interesting to see "Progressive" Democrat Congresswomen, who originally came from countries whose governments are a complete and total catastrophe, the worst, most corrupt and inept anywhere in the world (if they even have a functioning government at all), now loudly......

💬 69.6K   ⟲ 69.4K   ♡ 181.4K   ⬆

Donald J. Trump ✔ @realDonaldTrump · Jul 14, 2019 ooo

....and viciously telling the people of the United States, the greatest and most powerful Nation on earth, how our government is to be run. Why don't they go back and help fix the totally broken and crime infested places from which they came. Then come back and show us how....

💬 30.8K   ⟲ 44.8K   ♡ 159.8K   ⬆

Donald J. Trump ✔ @realDonaldTrump · Jul 14, 2019 ○○○

.....it is done. These places need your help badly, you can't leave fast enough. I'm sure that Nancy Pelosi would be very happy to quickly work out free travel arrangements!

  ◯ 31.6K   ⟲ 34K   ♡ 161.6K   ⬆

Donald J. Trump ✔ @realDonaldTrump · Jul 15, 2019 ○○○

We will never be a Socialist or Communist Country. IF YOU ARE NOT HAPPY HERE, YOU CAN LEAVE! It is your choice, and your choice alone. This is about love for America. Certain people HATE our Country....

  ◯ 60.6K   ⟲ 66.6K   ♡ 244.8K   ⬆

Donald J. Trump ✔ @realDonaldTrump · Jul 15, 2019 ○○○

.....They are anti-Israel, pro Al-Qaeda, and comment on the 9/11 attack, "some people did something." Radical Left Democrats want Open Borders, which means drugs, crime, human trafficking, and much more....

  ◯ 11.3K   ⟲ 28K   ♡ 133.4K   ⬆

Donald J. Trump ✔ @realDonaldTrump · Jul 15, 2019 ○○○

.....Detention facilities are not Concentration Camps! America has never been stronger than it is now – rebuilt Military, highest Stock Market EVER, lowest unemployment and more people working than ever before. Keep America Great!

  ◯ 15.8K   ⟲ 27.1K   ♡ 137.6K   ⬆

Donald J. Trump ✔ @realDonaldTrump · Jul 15, 2019 ○○○

The Obama Administration built the Cages, not the Trump Administration! DEMOCRATS MUST GIVE US THE VOTES TO CHANGE BAD IMMIGRATION LAWS.

  ◯ 25.8K   ⟲ 35.1K   ♡ 132.6K   ⬆

Donald J. Trump ✔ @realDonaldTrump · Jul 15, 2019 ○○○

MAKE AMERICA GREAT AGAIN!

  ◯ 58.5K   ⟲ 58.2K   ♡ 264.5K   ⬆

Donald J. Trump ✔ @realDonaldTrump · Jul 16, 2019 ○○○

Our Country is Free, Beautiful and Very Successful. If you hate our Country, or if you are not happy here, you can leave!

  ◯ 63.1K   ⟲ 78.8K   ♡ 293.9K   ⬆

Donald J. Trump ✔ @realDonaldTrump · Jul 19, 2019

Just spoke to @KanyeWest about his friend A$AP Rocky's incarceration. I will be calling the very talented Prime Minister of Sweden to see what we can do about helping A$AP Rocky. So many people would like to see this quickly resolved!

💬 49.3K   🔁 261.8K   ♡ 670.8K   ⬆

Donald J. Trump ✔ @realDonaldTrump · Jul 24, 2019

TRUTH IS A FORCE OF NATURE!

💬 54.3K   🔁 55.7K   ♡ 202.5K   ⬆

Donald J. Trump ✔ @realDonaldTrump · Jul 24, 2019

NO COLLUSION, NO OBSTRUCTION!

💬 27.8K   🔁 18.9K   ♡ 85.4K   ⬆

Donald J. Trump ✔ @realDonaldTrump · Jul 25, 2019

Give A$AP Rocky his FREEDOM. We do so much for Sweden but it doesn't seem to work the other way around. Sweden should focus on its real crime problem! #FreeRocky

💬 31.4K   🔁 115.2K   ♡ 299.9K   ⬆

Donald J. Trump ✔ @realDonaldTrump · Jul 26, 2019

France just put a digital tax on our great American technology companies. If anybody taxes them, it should be their home Country, the USA. We will announce a substantial reciprocal action on Macron's foolishness shortly. I've always said American wine is better than French wine!

💬 36.3K   🔁 52.1K   ♡ 161.9K   ⬆

Donald J. Trump ✔ @realDonaldTrump · Jul 27, 2019

Why is so much money sent to the Elijah Cummings district when it is considered the worst run and most dangerous anywhere in the United States. No human being would want to live there. Where is all this money going? How much is stolen? Investigate this corrupt mess immediately!

💬 48.2K   🔁 44.5K   ♡ 146.6K   ⬆

Donald J. Trump ✔ @realDonaldTrump · Jul 27, 2019

Consideration is being given to declaring ANTIFA, the gutless Radical Left Wack Jobs who go around hitting (only non-fighters) people over the heads with baseball bats, a major Organization of Terror (along with MS-13 & others). Would make it easier for police to do their job!

💬 26.9K   🔁 41.6K   ♡ 129.3K   ⬆

Donald J. Trump ✔ @realDonaldTrump · Jul 30, 2019   ⋯

We should immediately pass Voter ID @Voteridplease to insure the safety and sanctity of our voting system. Also, Paper Ballots as backup (old fashioned but true!). Thank you!

💬 15.1K   ⟲ 40K   ♡ 124.8K   ⬆

Donald J. Trump ✔ @realDonaldTrump · Aug 2, 2019   ⋯

Really bad news! The Baltimore house of Elijah Cummings was robbed. Too bad!

💬 65.8K   ⟲ 37.2K   ♡ 109K   ⬆

Donald J. Trump ✔ @realDonaldTrump · Aug 2, 2019   ⋯

A$AP Rocky released from prison and on his way home to the United States from Sweden. It was a Rocky Week, get home ASAP A$AP!

💬 35.3K   ⟲ 308.4K   ♡ 812.3K   ⬆

Donald J. Trump ✔ @realDonaldTrump · Aug 10, 2019   ⋯

Never has the press been more inaccurate, unfair or corrupt! We are not fighting the Democrats, they are easy, we are fighting the seriously dishonest and unhinged Lamestream Media. They have gone totally CRAZY. MAKE AMERICA GREAT AGAIN!

💬 36.8K   ⟲ 37.4K   ♡ 146.8K   ⬆

Donald J. Trump ✔ @realDonaldTrump · Aug 10, 2019   ⋯

Joe Biden just said, "We believe in facts, not truth." Does anybody really believe he is mentally fit to be president? We are "playing" in a very big and complicated world. Joe doesn't have a clue!

💬 49.6K   ⟲ 33.7K   ♡ 139.9K   ⬆

Donald J. Trump ✔ @realDonaldTrump · Aug 13, 2019   ⋯

No debate on Election Security should go forward without first agreeing that Voter ID (Identification) must play a very strong part in any final agreement. Without Voter ID, it is all so meaningless!

💬 20.5K   ⟲ 35.8K   ♡ 122.7K   ⬆

Donald J. Trump ✔ @realDonaldTrump · Aug 16, 2019   ⋯

Rep. Tlaib wrote a letter to Israeli officials desperately wanting to visit her grandmother. Permission was quickly granted, whereupon Tlaib obnoxiously turned the approval down, a complete setup. The only real winner here is Tlaib's grandmother. She doesn't have to see her now!

💬 40.8K   ⟲ 46.6K   ♡ 172.6K   ⬆

Donald J. Trump ✔ @realDonaldTrump · Aug 16, 2019

000

I donate 100% of my President's salary, $400,000, back to our Country, and feel very good about it!

> 🌐 **Judd Deere** ✔ @JuddPDeere45 · Aug 16, 2019
>
> #BREAKING @POTUS @realDonaldTrump has donated his 2019 second quarter salary to the Surgeon General's office | h/t @JayneODonnell @USATODAY | @Surgeon_General | usatoday.com/story/news/hea...

💬 32.6K   🔁 36.5K   ♡ 143K   ⬆️

Donald J. Trump ✔ @realDonaldTrump · Aug 18, 2019

000

MAKE AMERICA GREAT AGAIN!

💬 40.9K   🔁 45.2K   ♡ 224.7K   ⬆️

Donald J. Trump ✔ @realDonaldTrump · Aug 19, 2019

000

I promise not to do this to Greenland!

💬 38.2K   🔁 80K   ♡ 277.9K   ⬆️

Donald J. Trump ✓ @realDonaldTrump · Aug 20, 2019   ◦◦◦
Denmark is a very special country with incredible people, but based on Prime Minister Mette Frederiksen's comments, that she would have no interest in discussing the purchase of Greenland, I will be postponing our meeting scheduled in two weeks for another time....

💬 50K   🔁 38.4K   ♡ 101.2K   ⬆️

Donald J. Trump ✓ @realDonaldTrump · Aug 20, 2019   ◦◦◦
....The Prime Minister was able to save a great deal of expense and effort for both the United States and Denmark by being so direct. I thank her for that and look forward to rescheduling sometime in the future!

💬 16.3K   🔁 14.5K   ♡ 82.1K   ⬆️

Donald J. Trump ✓ @realDonaldTrump · Aug 23, 2019   ◦◦◦
94% Approval Rating within the Republican Party. Thank you!

💬 19.1K   🔁 20.7K   ♡ 115.8K   ⬆️

Donald J. Trump ✓ @realDonaldTrump · Aug 27, 2019   ◦◦◦
Axios (whatever that is) sat back and said GEEEEE, let's see, what can we make up today to embarrass the President? Then they said, "why don't we say he wants to bomb a hurricane, that should do it!" The media in our Country is totally out of control!

💬 20.4K   🔁 21.5K   ♡ 85K   ⬆️

Donald J. Trump ✓ @realDonaldTrump · Sep 12, 2019   ◦◦◦
"We can't beat him, so lets impeach him!" Democrat Rep. Al Green

💬 17.6K   🔁 21.2K   ♡ 84.5K   ⬆️

Donald J. Trump ✓ @realDonaldTrump · Sep 14, 2019   ◦◦◦
"A Very Stable Genius!" Thank you.

💬 26K   🔁 17.2K   ♡ 67.1K   ⬆️

Donald J. Trump ✓ @realDonaldTrump · Sep 14, 2019   ◦◦◦
MAKE AMERICA GREAT AGAIN!

💬 22.9K   🔁 38.9K   ♡ 207.9K   ⬆️

Donald J. Trump ✔ @realDonaldTrump · Sep 23, 2019
She seems like a very happy young girl looking forward to a bright and
wonderful future. So nice to see!

 **WIRED** ✔ @WIRED · Sep 23, 2019
"People are suffering, people are dying, entire ecosystems are collapsing.
We are in the beginning of a mass extinction and all you can talk about is
money and fairytales of eternal economic growth." Watch Greta Thunberg
speak at the UN Monday morning. wired.trib.al/VXdAnKt

Show this thread

💬 56K   ↻ 66.7K   ♡ 193.5K   ⬆

 Donald J. Trump ✔ @realDonaldTrump · Sep 26, 2019
Liddle' Adam Schiff, who has worked unsuccessfully for 3 years to hurt the
Republican Party and President, has just said that the Whistleblower, even
though he or she only had second hand information, "is credible." How can
that be with zero info and a known bias. Democrat Scam!

💬 39.4K   ↻ 29.5K   ♡ 106.9K   ⬆

 **Donald J. Trump** ✔ @realDonaldTrump · Sep 27, 2019
"IT WAS A PERFECT CONVERSATION WITH UKRAINE PRESIDENT!"

💬 21.5K   ↻ 16K   ♡ 70.8K   ⬆

Donald J. Trump ✔ @realDonaldTrump · Sep 27, 2019
Rep. Adam Schiff totally made up my conversation with Ukraine President and
read it to Congress and Millions. He must resign and be investigated. He has
been doing this for two years. He is a sick man!

💬 24.2K   ↻ 33.8K   ♡ 112.4K   ⬆

Donald J. Trump ✔ @realDonaldTrump · Oct 1, 2019   ooo

Try to impeach this.

◯ 60.7K   ⟲ 87.5K   ♡ 215K   ⬆

Donald J. Trump ✔ @realDonaldTrump · Oct 1, 2019   ooo
As I learn more and more each day, I am coming to the conclusion that what
is taking place is not an impeachment, it is a COUP, intended to take away the
Power of the....

◯ 42.3K   ⟲ 48.8K   ♡ 149.3K   ⬆

Donald J. Trump ✔ @realDonaldTrump · Oct 1, 2019   ooo
....People, their VOTE, their Freedoms, their Second Amendment, Religion,
Military, Border Wall, and their God-given rights as a Citizen of The United
States of America!

◯ 26K   ⟲ 30.9K   ♡ 114.6K   ⬆

Donald J. Trump ✔ @realDonaldTrump · Oct 4, 2019   ooo
As President I have an obligation to end CORRUPTION, even if that means
requesting the help of a foreign country or countries. It is done all the time.
This has NOTHING to do with politics or a political campaign against the
Bidens. This does have to do with their corruption!

◯ 49.6K   ⟲ 38.9K   ♡ 132.3K   ⬆

 Donald J. Trump ✔ @realDonaldTrump · Oct 4, 2019   ooo
Breaking News: Unemployment Rate, at 3.5%, drops to a 50 YEAR LOW. Wow
America, lets impeach your President (even though he did nothing wrong!).

◯ 22K   ⟲ 37K   ♡ 149.2K   ⬆

Donald J. Trump ✔ @realDonaldTrump · Oct 5, 2019   ⬤⬤⬤

Mitt Romney never knew how to win. He is a pompous "ass" who has been fighting me from the beginning, except when he begged me for my endorsement for his Senate run (I gave it to him), and when he begged me to be Secretary of State (I didn't give it to him). He is so bad for R's!

💬 38.2K   🔁 37.3K   ♡ 125.2K   ⬆

Donald J. Trump ✔ @realDonaldTrump · Oct 6, 2019   ⬤⬤⬤

DRAIN THE SWAMP!

💬 29.7K   🔁 31.6K   ♡ 128.3K   ⬆

Donald J. Trump ✔ @realDonaldTrump · Oct 6, 2019   ⬤⬤⬤

Unemployment Rate just dropped to 3.5%, the lowest in more that 50 years. Is that an impeachable event for your President?

💬 29K   🔁 33K   ♡ 157K   ⬆

Donald J. Trump ✔ @realDonaldTrump · Oct 7, 2019   ⬤⬤⬤

We just WON the big court case on Net Neutrality Rules! A great win for the future and speed of the internet. Will lead to many big things including 5G. Congratulations to the FCC and its Chairman, Ajit Pai!

💬 7.3K   🔁 16.4K   ♡ 68.2K   ⬆

Donald J. Trump ✔ @realDonaldTrump · Oct 9, 2019   ⬤⬤⬤

The United States has spent EIGHT TRILLION DOLLARS fighting and policing in the Middle East. Thousands of our Great Soldiers have died or been badly wounded. Millions of people have died on the other side. GOING INTO THE MIDDLE EAST IS THE WORST DECISION EVER MADE.....

💬 11.9K   🔁 27K   ♡ 92.3K   ⬆

Donald J. Trump ✔ @realDonaldTrump · Oct 9, 2019   ⬤⬤⬤

....IN THE HISTORY OF OUR COUNTRY! We went to war under a false & now disproven premise, WEAPONS OF MASS DESTRUCTION. There were NONE! Now we are slowly & carefully bringing our great soldiers & military home. Our focus is on the BIG PICTURE! THE USA IS GREATER THAN EVER BEFORE!

💬 8.2K   🔁 17.9K   ♡ 67.8K   ⬆

Donald J. Trump ✔ @realDonaldTrump · Oct 11, 2019   ⬤⬤⬤

WHERE'S HUNTER?

💬 36K   🔁 37K   ♡ 110.9K   ⬆

Donald J. Trump ✔ @realDonaldTrump · Oct 12, 2019   ⬤⬤⬤

The Endless Wars Must End!

💬 36.8K   🔁 31.3K   ♡ 125K   ⬆

Donald J. Trump ✔ @realDonaldTrump · Oct 16, 2019

Senator Rand Paul just wrote a great book, "The Case Against Socialism" which is now out. Highly recommended – as America was founded on LIBERTY & INDEPENDENCE – not government coercion, domination & control. We were born free, and will stay free, as long as I am your President!

💬 14.6K   ↻ 21.9K   ♡ 83.7K   ⬆️

Donald J. Trump ✔ @realDonaldTrump · Oct 16, 2019

Nancy Pelosi needs help fast! There is either something wrong with her "upstairs," or she just plain doesn't like our great Country. She had a total meltdown in the White House today. It was very sad to watch. Pray for her, she is a very sick person!

💬 62.5K   ↻ 50K   ♡ 167.4K   ⬆️

Donald J. Trump ✔ @realDonaldTrump · Oct 19, 2019

So now Crooked Hillary is at it again! She is calling Congresswoman Tulsi Gabbard "a Russian favorite," and Jill Stein "a Russian asset." As you may have heard, I was called a big Russia lover also (actually, I do like Russian people. I like all people!). Hillary's gone Crazy!

💬 29.4K   ↻ 34.6K   ♡ 147K   ⬆️

Donald J. Trump ✔ @realDonaldTrump · Oct 23, 2019

The Never Trumper Republicans, though on respirators with not many left, are in certain ways worse and more dangerous for our Country than the Do Nothing Democrats. Watch out for them, they are human scum!

💬 41.6K   ↻ 32.4K   ♡ 90.4K   ⬆️

Donald J. Trump ✔ @realDonaldTrump · Oct 28, 2019

We have declassified a picture of the wonderful dog (name not declassified) that did such a GREAT JOB in capturing and killing the Leader of ISIS, Abu Bakr al-Baghdadi!

💬 50.1K   ↻ 140.9K   ♡ 518.8K   ⬆️

Donald J. Trump ✔ @realDonaldTrump · Oct 29, 2019   ⚬⚬⚬

Just confirmed that Abu Bakr al-Baghdadi's number one replacement has been terminated by American troops. Most likely would have taken the top spot - Now he is also Dead!

💬 19.6K   ⟲ 49.2K   ♡ 223K   ⬆

Donald J. Trump ✔ @realDonaldTrump · Oct 30, 2019   ⚬⚬⚬

AMERICAN HERO!

@realDailyWire

💬 48.2K   ⟲ 101K   ♡ 399.4K   ⬆

Donald J. Trump ✔ @realDonaldTrump · Oct 31, 2019   ⚬⚬⚬

1600 Pennsylvania Avenue, the White House, is the place I have come to love and will stay for, hopefully, another 5 years as we MAKE AMERICA GREAT AGAIN, but my family and I will be making Palm Beach, Florida, our Permanent Residence. I cherish New York, and the people of.....

💬 20.3K   ⟲ 23.6K   ♡ 97.9K   ⬆

Donald J. Trump ✔ @realDonaldTrump · Oct 31, 2019   ○○○
....New York, and always will, but unfortunately, despite the fact that I pay millions of dollars in city, state and local taxes each year, I have been treated very badly by the political leaders of both the city and state. Few have been treated worse. I hated having to make....

  💬 6.7K　　　🔁 13.8K　　　♡ 67.2K　　　🔗

Donald J. Trump ✔ @realDonaldTrump · Oct 31, 2019   ○○○
....this decision, but in the end it will be best for all concerned. As President, I will always be there to help New York and the great people of New York. It will always have a special place in my heart!

  💬 12.1K　　　🔁 14K　　　♡ 71.2K　　　🔗

Donald J. Trump ✔ @realDonaldTrump · Nov 1, 2019   ○○○
ISIS has a new leader. We know exactly who he is!

  💬 46.1K　　　🔁 53.3K　　　♡ 217.7K　　　🔗

Donald J. Trump ✔ @realDonaldTrump · Nov 1, 2019   ○○○
Oh no, Beto just dropped out of race for President despite him saying he was "born for this." I don't think so!

  💬 22.7K　　　🔁 33.3K　　　♡ 168.4K　　　🔗

Donald J. Trump ✔ @realDonaldTrump · Nov 1, 2019   ○○○
You can't Impeach someone who hasn't done anything wrong!

  💬 63.8K　　　🔁 56.9K　　　♡ 257.1K　　　🔗

Donald J. Trump ✔ @realDonaldTrump · Nov 2, 2019   ○○○
The Whistleblower has disappeared. Where is the Whistleblower?

  💬 34K　　　🔁 31.2K　　　♡ 131.4K　　　🔗

Donald J. Trump ✔ @realDonaldTrump · Nov 4, 2019   ○○○
Stock Market hits RECORD HIGH. Spend your money well!

  💬 10.6K　　　🔁 22.3K　　　♡ 110.4K　　　🔗

Donald J. Trump ✔ @realDonaldTrump · Nov 7, 2019   ○○○
Years ago, when Media was legitimate, people known as "Fact Checkers" would always call to check and see if a story was accurate. Nowadays they don't use "Fact Checkers" anymore, they just write whatever they want!

  💬 23.5K　　　🔁 23.9K　　　♡ 99.4K　　　🔗

Donald J. Trump ✔ @realDonaldTrump · Nov 7, 2019   ○○○
Stock Market up big today. A New Record. Enjoy!

  💬 16.6K　　　🔁 18.4K　　　♡ 100.7K　　　🔗

Donald J. Trump ✔ @realDonaldTrump · Nov 10, 2019 ⚬⚬⚬
The call to the Ukrainian President was PERFECT. Read the Transcript! There was NOTHING said that was in any way wrong. Republicans, don't be led into the fools trap of saying it was not perfect, but is not impeachable. No, it is much stronger than that. NOTHING WAS DONE WRONG!

💬 31.7K   ⟲ 22K   ♡ 85.3K   ⬆

Donald J. Trump ✔ @realDonaldTrump · Nov 10, 2019 ⚬⚬⚬
If Iran is able to turn over to the U.S. kidnapped former FBI Agent Robert A. Levinson, who has been missing in Iran for 12 years, it would be a very positive step. At the same time, upon information & belief, Iran is, & has been, enriching uranium. THAT WOULD BE A VERY BAD STEP!

💬 6.4K   ⟲ 16.5K   ♡ 65.5K   ⬆

Donald J. Trump ✔ @realDonaldTrump · Nov 11, 2019 ⚬⚬⚬
HAPPY VETERANS DAY!

💬 15.9K   ⟲ 27.6K   ♡ 149.5K   ⬆

Donald J. Trump ✔ @realDonaldTrump · Nov 11, 2019 ⚬⚬⚬
In order to continue being the most Transparent President in history, I will be releasing sometime this week the Transcript of the first, and therefore most important, phone call I had with the President of Ukraine. I am sure you will find it tantalizing!

💬 39.9K   ⟲ 31.9K   ♡ 113.7K   ⬆

Donald J. Trump ✔ @realDonaldTrump · Nov 13, 2019 ⚬⚬⚬
Wow! Was just told that my son's book, "Triggered," is Number One on The New York Times Bestseller List. Congratulations Don!

💬 25.5K   ⟲ 24.9K   ♡ 144.2K   ⬆

Donald J. Trump ✔ @realDonaldTrump · Nov 16, 2019 ⚬⚬⚬
Dow hits 28,000 - FIRST TIME EVER, HIGHEST EVER! Gee, Pelosi & Schitt have a good idea, "lets Impeach the President." If something like that ever happened, it would lead to the biggest FALL in Market History. It's called a Depression, not a Recession! So much for 401-K's & Jobs!

💬 27.6K   ⟲ 27.7K   ♡ 104.9K   ⬆

Donald J. Trump ✔ @realDonaldTrump · Nov 19, 2019 ⚬⚬⚬
NASDAQ UP 27% THIS YEAR ALONE!

💬 17.1K   ⟲ 18.7K   ♡ 92.9K   ⬆

Donald J. Trump ✔ @realDonaldTrump · Nov 20, 2019 ⚬⚬⚬
If this were a prizefight, they'd stop it!

💬 29.6K   ⟲ 24K   ♡ 108.8K   ⬆

Donald J. Trump ✓ @realDonaldTrump · Nov 26, 2019 ○○○
I will always protect our great warfighters. I've got your backs!

💬 23.7K   🔁 27.8K   ♡ 140.6K   ⬆

 Donald J. Trump ✓ @realDonaldTrump · Nov 27, 2019 ○○○

💬 145.4K   🔁 278.9K   ♡ 637.6K   ⬆

 Donald J. Trump ✓ @realDonaldTrump · Nov 27, 2019 ○○○
95% Approval Rating in the Republican Party. Thank you!

💬 23.4K   🔁 25.7K   ♡ 158.5K   ⬆

Donald J. Trump ✔ @realDonaldTrump · Dec 5, 2019 ○○○
Where's the Fake Whistleblower? Where's Whistleblower number 2? Where's the phony informer who got it all wrong?

💬 29.3K   🔁 28.7K   ♡ 120.5K   ⬆

Donald J. Trump ✔ @realDonaldTrump · Dec 6, 2019 ○○○
Do not believe any article or story you read or see that uses "anonymous sources" having to do with trade or any other subject. Only accept information if it has an actual living name on it. The Fake News Media makes up many "sources say" stories. Do not believe them!

💬 32K   🔁 37.6K   ♡ 138.4K   ⬆

Donald J. Trump ✔ @realDonaldTrump · Dec 7, 2019 ○○○
The United States will not rest until we bring every American wrongfully detained in Iran and around the world back home to their loved ones!

> 🏛 **U.S. Embassy Bern** ✔ @USEmbassyBern · Dec 7, 2019
> Thank you to the Swiss (@SwissMFA) for helping President Trump (@POTUS) deliver on his commitment to bringing all Americans home. @freeXiyueWang (1/2)
>
>

💬 2.9K   🔁 15.8K   ♡ 60.1K   ⬆

Donald J. Trump ✔ @realDonaldTrump · Dec 7, 2019 ○○○
Our Economy is the envy of the World!

💬 16.4K   🔁 23.1K   ♡ 121.2K   ⬆

Donald J. Trump ✔ @realDonaldTrump · Dec 9, 2019 ○○○
Read the Transcripts!

💬 32.1K   🔁 22.2K   ♡ 101.8K   ⬆

Donald J. Trump ✔ @realDonaldTrump · Dec 12, 2019   ⋯

So ridiculous. Greta must work on her Anger Management problem, then go to a good old fashioned movie with a friend! Chill Greta, Chill!

> **Roma Downey** ✔ @RealRomaDowney · Dec 11, 2019
> Congrats @GretaThunberg twitter.com/TIME/status/12...

💬 113.4K   ♻ 104.3K   ♡ 203.7K   ⬆

Donald J. Trump ✔ @realDonaldTrump · Dec 12, 2019   ⋯

#ThrowbackThursday🇺🇸

💬 7.2K   ♻ 16.8K   ♡ 72.4K   ⬆

Donald J. Trump ✔ @realDonaldTrump · Dec 13, 2019   ⋯

Congratulations to Boris Johnson on his great WIN! Britain and the United States will now be free to strike a massive new Trade Deal after BREXIT. This deal has the potential to be far bigger and more lucrative than any deal that could be made with the E.U. Celebrate Boris!

💬 13.5K   ♻ 53K   ♡ 177K   ⬆

Donald J. Trump ✔ @realDonaldTrump · Dec 16, 2019   ⋯

New Stock Market high! I will never get bored of telling you that – and we will never get tired of winning!

💬 20K   ♻ 31.6K   ♡ 145.3K   ⬆

Donald J. Trump ✔ @realDonaldTrump · Dec 18, 2019   ⋯

Can you believe that I will be impeached today by the Radical Left, Do Nothing Democrats, AND I DID NOTHING WRONG! A terrible Thing. Read the Transcripts. This should never happen to another President again. Say a PRAYER!

💬 93K   ♻ 95.8K   ♡ 216.6K   ⬆

Donald J. Trump ✔ @realDonaldTrump · Dec 18, 2019 ⋯

💬 82.2K　　🔁 143.9K　　♡ 416.2K　　⬆

 Donald J. Trump ✔ @realDonaldTrump · Dec 19, 2019 ⋯
PRESIDENTIAL HARASSMENT!

💬 39.3K　　🔁 54K　　♡ 178.7K　　⬆

Donald J. Trump ✓ @realDonaldTrump · Dec 19, 2019 ⋯

I got Impeached last night without one Republican vote being cast with the Do Nothing Dems on their continuation of the greatest Witch Hunt in American history. Now the Do Nothing Party want to Do Nothing with the Articles & not deliver them to the Senate, but it's Senate's call!

💬 21.2K　　　🔁 28K　　　♡ 124.6K　　　⬆️

Donald J. Trump ✓ @realDonaldTrump · Dec 19, 2019 ⋯

So after the Democrats gave me no Due Process in the House, no lawyers, no witnesses, no nothing, they now want to tell the Senate how to run their trial. Actually, they have zero proof of anything, they will never even show up. They want out. I want an immediate trial!

💬 34.7K　　　🔁 42.5K　　　♡ 186.2K　　　⬆️

Donald J. Trump ✓ @realDonaldTrump · Dec 20, 2019 ⋯

Nancy Pelosi is looking for a Quid Pro Quo with the Senate. Why aren't we Impeaching her?

💬 45.7K　　　🔁 47.7K　　　♡ 181.9K　　　⬆️

Donald J. Trump ✓ @realDonaldTrump · Dec 20, 2019 ⋯

Broke all time Stock Market Record again today. 135 times since my 2016 Election Win. Thank you!

💬 11.6K　　　🔁 25.2K　　　♡ 137.3K　　　⬆️

Donald J. Trump ✓ @realDonaldTrump · Dec 25, 2019 ⋯

MERRY CHRISTMAS!

💬 74.9K　　　🔁 109.1K　　　♡ 671.9K　　　⬆️

Donald J. Trump ✓ @realDonaldTrump · Dec 26, 2019 ⋯

I guess Justin T doesn't much like my making him pay up on NATO or Trade!

> 🦊 **FOX 13 Tampa Bay** ✓ @FOX13News · Dec 26, 2019
>
> President Trump's cameo in "Home Alone 2: Lost In New York" was reportedly cut from showings of the movie on Canadian broadcasts. The network says it was to make room for commercials. bit.ly/2SuSSi2

💬 18.3K　　　🔁 20.6K　　　♡ 79.1K　　　⬆️

Donald J. Trump ✓ @realDonaldTrump · Dec 31, 2019 ⋯

HAPPY NEW YEAR!

💬 51.5K　　　🔁 81.8K　　　♡ 522.3K　　　⬆️

Donald J. Trump ✔ @realDonaldTrump · Jan 2, 2020   ⦁⦁⦁

💬 164.2K   ⟲ 212.4K   ♡ 738.7K   ⬆️

Donald J. Trump ✔ @realDonaldTrump · Jan 3, 2020   ⦁⦁⦁
Iran never won a war, but never lost a negotiation!

💬 38.3K   ⟲ 79.3K   ♡ 296.3K   ⬆️

Donald J. Trump ✔ @realDonaldTrump · Jan 3, 2020   ⦁⦁⦁
General Qassem Soleimani has killed or badly wounded thousands of
Americans over an extended period of time, and was plotting to kill many
more...but got caught! He was directly and indirectly responsible for the
death of millions of people, including the recent large number....

💬 24.7K   ⟲ 52K   ♡ 219.8K   ⬆️

Donald J. Trump ✔ @realDonaldTrump · Jan 3, 2020   ⦁⦁⦁
....of PROTESTERS killed in Iran itself. While Iran will never be able to properly
admit it, Soleimani was both hated and feared within the country. They are not
nearly as saddened as the leaders will let the outside world believe. He
should have been taken out many years ago!

💬 10K   ⟲ 27.8K   ♡ 126.9K   ⬆️

Donald J. Trump ✔ @realDonaldTrump · Jan 5, 2020   ⦁⦁⦁
The United States just spent Two Trillion Dollars on Military Equipment. We
are the biggest and by far the BEST in the World! If Iran attacks an American
Base, or any American, we will be sending some of that brand new beautiful
equipment their way...and without hesitation!

💬 111K   ⟲ 220.6K   ♡ 625.6K   ⬆️

Donald J. Trump ✔ @realDonaldTrump · Jan 5, 2020

These Media Posts will serve as notification to the United States Congress that should Iran strike any U.S. person or target, the United States will quickly & fully strike back, & perhaps in a disproportionate manner. Such legal notice is not required, but is given nevertheless!

💬 95.2K   🔁 102.4K   ♡ 342.1K   ↥

Donald J. Trump ✔ @realDonaldTrump · Jan 6, 2020

IRAN WILL NEVER HAVE A NUCLEAR WEAPON!

💬 74.7K   🔁 105.7K   ♡ 428.7K   ↥

Donald J. Trump ✔ @realDonaldTrump · Jan 7, 2020

All is well! Missiles launched from Iran at two military bases located in Iraq. Assessment of casualties & damages taking place now. So far, so good! We have the most powerful and well equipped military anywhere in the world, by far! I will be making a statement tomorrow morning.

💬 140.4K   🔁 192.5K   ♡ 699.8K   ↥

Donald J. Trump ✔ @realDonaldTrump · Jan 11, 2020

Nancy Pelosi will go down as the absolute worst Speaker of the House in U.S. history!

💬 28.4K   🔁 35.7K   ♡ 191.2K   ↥

Donald J. Trump ✔ @realDonaldTrump · Jan 11, 2020

به مردم شجاع و رنج کشیده ایران: من از ابتدای دوره ریاست جمهوریم با شما ایستاده‌ام و دولت من همچنان با شما خواهد ایستاد. ما اعتراضات شما را از نزدیک دنبال می کنیم. شجاعت شما الهام بخش است.

💬 44.1K   🔁 105K   ♡ 336.6K   ↥

Donald J. Trump ✔ @realDonaldTrump · Jan 11, 2020

The government of Iran must allow human rights groups to monitor and report facts from the ground on the ongoing protests by the Iranian people. There can not be another massacre of peaceful protesters, nor an internet shutdown. The world is watching.

💬 15.5K   🔁 41.7K   ♡ 173K   ↥

Donald J. Trump ✔ @realDonaldTrump · Jan 12, 2020

To the leaders of Iran - DO NOT KILL YOUR PROTESTERS. Thousands have already been killed or imprisoned by you, and the World is watching. More importantly, the USA is watching. Turn your internet back on and let reporters roam free! Stop the killing of your great Iranian people!

💬 31.8K   🔁 106.3K   ♡ 309.7K   ↥

Donald J. Trump ✔ @realDonaldTrump · Jan 13, 2020   ⚬⚬⚬

Really Big Breaking News (Kidding): Booker, who was in zero polling territory, just dropped out of the Democrat Presidential Primary Race. Now I can rest easy tonight. I was sooo concerned that I would someday have to go head to head with him!

💬 35.7K   ⟳ 33.3K   ♡ 152.5K   ⬆️

Donald J. Trump ✔ @realDonaldTrump · Jan 13, 2020   ⚬⚬⚬

I stand stronger than anyone in protecting your Healthcare with Pre-Existing Conditions. I am honored to have terminated the very unfair, costly and unpopular individual mandate for you!

💬 40.3K   ⟳ 35.3K   ♡ 189K   ⬆️

Donald J. Trump ✔ @realDonaldTrump · Jan 16, 2020   ⚬⚬⚬

I JUST GOT IMPEACHED FOR MAKING A PERFECT PHONE CALL!

💬 99.5K   ⟳ 82.3K   ♡ 316.1K   ⬆️

Donald J. Trump ✔ @realDonaldTrump · Jan 20, 2020   ⚬⚬⚬

USA! USA! USA!

💬 34.4K   ⟳ 83K   ♡ 291.7K   ⬆️

Donald J. Trump ✔ @realDonaldTrump · Jan 21, 2020   ⚬⚬⚬

READ THE TRANSCRIPTS!

💬 45K   ⟳ 33K   ♡ 156.1K   ⬆️

Donald J. Trump ✔ @realDonaldTrump · Jan 23, 2020   ⚬⚬⚬

💬 48.9K   ⟳ 100.9K   ♡ 318.2K   ⬆️

Donald J. Trump ✔ @realDonaldTrump · Jan 30, 2020   ooo

BIGGEST TRADE DEAL EVER MADE, the USMCA, was signed yesterday and the Fake News Media barely mentioned it. They never thought it could be done. They have zero credibility!

🗨 14.9K   ⟲ 29.1K   ♡ 130.9K   ⬆

Donald J. Trump ✔ @realDonaldTrump · Jan 30, 2020   ooo

Working closely with China and others on Coronavirus outbreak. Only 5 people in U.S., all in good recovery.

🗨 10.9K   ⟲ 21.5K   ♡ 124.1K   ⬆

Donald J. Trump ✔ @realDonaldTrump · Jan 31, 2020   ooo

The Radical Left, Do Nothing Democrats keep chanting "fairness", when they put on the most unfair Witch Hunt in the history of the U.S. Congress. They had 17 Witnesses, we were allowed ZERO, and no lawyers. They didn't do their job, had no case. The Dems are scamming America!

🗨 35.6K   ⟲ 41.2K   ♡ 163K   ⬆

Donald J. Trump ✔ @realDonaldTrump · Jan 31, 2020   ooo

No matter what you give to the Democrats, in the end, they will NEVER be satisfied. In the House, they gave us NOTHING!

🗨 26.6K   ⟲ 34.4K   ♡ 172.9K   ⬆

Donald J. Trump ✔ @realDonaldTrump · Feb 1, 2020   ooo

Getting a little exercise this morning!

🗨 52.2K   ⟲ 38.3K   ♡ 278.5K   ⬆

Donald J. Trump ✔ @realDonaldTrump · Feb 2, 2020

Mini Mike is now negotiating both to get on the Democrat Primary debate stage, and to have the right to stand on boxes, or a lift, during the debates. This is sometimes done, but really not fair!

💬 33.8K   🔁 25.5K   ♡ 106.6K   ⬆️

Donald J. Trump ✔ @realDonaldTrump · Feb 8, 2020

Pete Rose played Major League Baseball for 24 seasons, from 1963-1986, and had more hits, 4,256, than any other player (by a wide margin). He gambled, but only on his own team winning, and paid a decades long price. GET PETE ROSE INTO THE BASEBALL HALL OF FAME. It's Time!

💬 20.7K   🔁 51.5K   ♡ 199.9K   ⬆️

Donald J. Trump ✔ @realDonaldTrump · Feb 13, 2020

DRAIN THE SWAMP! We want bad people out of our government!

💬 75.5K   🔁 56.3K   ♡ 217.3K   ⬆️

Donald J. Trump ✔ @realDonaldTrump · Feb 13, 2020

I'm seeing Governor Cuomo today at The White House. He must understand that National Security far exceeds politics. New York must stop all of its unnecessary lawsuits & harrassment, start cleaning itself up, and lowering taxes. Build relationships, but don't bring Fredo!

💬 37.6K   🔁 36K   ♡ 139.6K   ⬆️

Donald J. Trump ✔ @realDonaldTrump · Feb 17, 2020

HAPPY PRESIDENT'S DAY!

💬 49.4K   🔁 50.1K   ♡ 332.1K   ⬆️

Donald J. Trump ✔ @realDonaldTrump · Feb 24, 2020

मैं इसी लिए भारत आया हूँ, सद्भावना और प्रेम के साथ ताकि हम अपनी अभिलाषा प्रतीक अपनी सांझेदारी और अविश्वसनीय विस्तार सकें।

💬 5.9K   🔁 25.9K   ♡ 150.4K   ⬆️

Donald J. Trump ✔ @realDonaldTrump · Feb 24, 2020

The Coronavirus is very much under control in the USA. We are in contact with everyone and all relevant countries. CDC & World Health have been working hard and very smart. Stock Market starting to look very good to me!

💬 34.5K   🔁 50.4K   ♡ 131.7K   ⬆️

Donald J. Trump ✔ @realDonaldTrump · Feb 28, 2020

So, the Coronavirus, which started in China and spread to various countries throughout the world, but very slowly in the U.S. because President Trump closed our border, and ended flights, VERY EARLY, is now being blamed, by the Do Nothing Democrats, to be the fault of "Trump".

💬 31.1K   🔁 35.5K   ♡ 143.2K   ⬆️

Donald J. Trump ✔ @realDonaldTrump · Mar 2, 2020

They are staging a coup against Bernie!

💬 22.6K   🔁 30.2K   ♡ 133.6K   ⬆️

Donald J. Trump ✔ @realDonaldTrump · Mar 3, 2020

The biggest loser tonight, by far, is Mini Mike Bloomberg. His "political" consultants took him for a ride. $700 million washed down the drain, and he got nothing for it but the nickname Mini Mike, and the complete destruction of his reputation. Way to go Mike!

💬 18.2K   🔁 31.8K   ♡ 147.5K   ⬆️

Donald J. Trump ✔ @realDonaldTrump · Mar 3, 2020

Elizabeth "Pocahontas" Warren, other than Mini Mike, was the loser of the night. She didn't even come close to winning her home state of Massachusetts. Well, now she can just sit back with her husband and have a nice cold beer!

💬 21K   🔁 33.9K   ♡ 153.2K   ⬆️

Donald J. Trump ✔ @realDonaldTrump · Mar 4, 2020

Mini Mike Bloomberg just "quit" the race for President. I could have told him long ago that he didn't have what it takes, and he would have saved himself a billion dollars, the real cost. Now he will pour money into Sleepy Joe's campaign, hoping to save face. It won't work!

💬 18.4K   🔁 27.8K   ♡ 131.7K   ⬆️

Donald J. Trump ✔ @realDonaldTrump · Mar 4, 2020

There can be few things worse in a civilized, law abiding nation, than a United States Senator openly, and for all to see and hear, threatening the Supreme Court or its Justices. This is what Chuck Schumer just did. He must pay a severe price for this!

💬 28.5K   🔁 41.4K   ♡ 143.1K   ⬆️

Donald J. Trump ✔ @realDonaldTrump · Mar 5, 2020 ⋯
With approximately 100,000 CoronaVirus cases worldwide, and 3,280 deaths, the United States, because of quick action on closing our borders, has, as of now, only 129 cases (40 Americans brought in) and 11 deaths. We are working very hard to keep these numbers as low as possible!

💬 25.6K   ⟲ 27.5K   ♡ 126.7K   ⬆

Donald J. Trump ✔ @realDonaldTrump · Mar 8, 2020 ⋯
The New York Times is an embarrassment to journalism. They were a dead paper before I went into politics, and they will be a dead paper after I leave, which will be in 5 years. Fake News is the Enemy of the people!

💬 29.6K   ⟲ 38.3K   ♡ 167.3K   ⬆

Donald J. Trump ✔ @realDonaldTrump · Mar 9, 2020 ⋯
The Obama/Biden Administration is the most corrupt Administration in the history of our Country!

💬 56.2K   ⟲ 53.7K   ♡ 166.6K   ⬆

Donald J. Trump ✔ @realDonaldTrump · Mar 11, 2020 ⋯
Someone needs to tell the Democrats in Congress that CoronaVirus doesn't care what party you are in. We need to protect ALL Americans!

💬 20.8K   ⟲ 34.3K   ♡ 148.8K   ⬆

Donald J. Trump ✔ @realDonaldTrump · Mar 11, 2020 ⋯
I am fully prepared to use the full power of the Federal Government to deal with our current challenge of the CoronaVirus!

💬 29K   ⟲ 30.8K   ♡ 141K   ⬆

Donald J. Trump ✔ @realDonaldTrump · Mar 11, 2020 ⋯
The Media should view this as a time of unity and strength. We have a common enemy, actually, an enemy of the World, the CoronaVirus. We must beat it as quickly and safely as possible. There is nothing more important to me than the life & safety of the United States!

💬 43.3K   ⟲ 49.9K   ♡ 231.3K   ⬆

Donald J. Trump ✔ @realDonaldTrump · Mar 14, 2020 ⋯
BIGGEST STOCK MARKET RISE IN HISTORY YESTERDAY!

💬 38.8K   ⟲ 36.6K   ♡ 166.4K   ⬆

Donald J. Trump ✔ @realDonaldTrump · Mar 14, 2020 ⋯
SOCIAL DISTANCING!

💬 30.5K   ⟲ 59.3K   ♡ 211.9K   ⬆

Donald J. Trump ✔ @realDonaldTrump · Mar 15, 2020

TODAY IS A NATIONAL DAY OF PRAYER. GOD BLESS EVERYONE!

💬 33.2K 🔁 76.5K ♡ 376.5K ⬆️

Donald J. Trump ✔ @realDonaldTrump · Mar 15, 2020

So now it is reported that, after destroying his life & the life of his wonderful family (and many others also), the FBI, working in conjunction with the Justice Department, has "lost" the records of General Michael Flynn. How convenient. I am strongly considering a Full Pardon!

💬 55.1K 🔁 66.6K ♡ 211.5K ⬆️

Donald J. Trump ✔ @realDonaldTrump · Mar 16, 2020

God Bless the USA!

💬 43.2K 🔁 70.4K ♡ 398.2K ⬆️

Donald J. Trump ✔ @realDonaldTrump · Mar 16, 2020

Everybody is so well unified and working so hard. It is a beautiful thing to see. They love our great Country. We will end up being stronger than ever before!

💬 29.4K 🔁 34.1K ♡ 183.3K ⬆️

Donald J. Trump ✔ @realDonaldTrump · Mar 17, 2020

The world is at war with a hidden enemy. WE WILL WIN!

💬 64.7K 🔁 120.6K ♡ 520.9K ⬆️

Donald J. Trump ✔ @realDonaldTrump · Mar 19, 2020

We are going to WIN, sooner rather than later!

💬 36.6K 🔁 56.4K ♡ 316.6K ⬆️

Donald J. Trump ✔ @realDonaldTrump · Mar 22, 2020

WE CANNOT LET THE CURE BE WORSE THAN THE PROBLEM ITSELF. AT THE END OF THE 15 DAY PERIOD, WE WILL MAKE A DECISION AS TO WHICH WAY WE WANT TO GO!

💬 67.9K 🔁 71.5K ♡ 294.2K ⬆️

Donald J. Trump ✔ @realDonaldTrump · Mar 23, 2020

THIS IS WHY WE NEED BORDERS!

💬 55.6K 🔁 76.2K ♡ 357.9K ⬆️

Donald J. Trump ✔ @realDonaldTrump · Apr 5, 2020

We are learning much about the Invisible Enemy. It is tough and smart, but we are tougher and smarter!

💬 56.5K 🔁 66.4K ♡ 354.2K ⬆️

Donald J. Trump ✓ @realDonaldTrump · Apr 6, 2020
LIGHT AT THE END OF THE TUNNEL!

💬 53.7K　　⟲ 85.7K　　♡ 384.6K　　⬆️

Donald J. Trump ✓ @realDonaldTrump · Apr 7, 2020
The W.H.O. really blew it. For some reason, funded largely by the United States, yet very China centric. We will be giving that a good look. Fortunately I rejected their advice on keeping our borders open to China early on. Why did they give us such a faulty recommendation?

💬 75.6K　　⟲ 117.5K　　♡ 426.4K　　⬆️

Donald J. Trump ✓ @realDonaldTrump · Apr 8, 2020
Bernie Sanders is OUT! Thank you to Elizabeth Warren. If not for her, Bernie would have won almost every state on Super Tuesday! This ended just like the Democrats & the DNC wanted, same as the Crooked Hillary fiasco. The Bernie people should come to the Republican Party, TRADE!

💬 40.4K　　⟲ 78.9K　　♡ 260.5K　　⬆️

Donald J. Trump ✓ @realDonaldTrump · Apr 8, 2020
Absentee Ballots are a great way to vote for the many senior citizens, military, and others who can't get to the polls on Election Day. These ballots are very different from 100% Mail-In Voting, which is "RIPE for FRAUD," and shouldn't be allowed!

💬 44.5K　　⟲ 50.2K　　♡ 178.1K　　⬆️

Donald J. Trump ✓ @realDonaldTrump · Apr 10, 2020
The Invisible Enemy will soon be in full retreat!

💬 54.7K　　⟲ 84.6K　　♡ 411.6K　　⬆️

Donald J. Trump ✓ @realDonaldTrump · Apr 11, 2020
Mail in ballots substantially increases the risk of crime and VOTER FRAUD!

💬 43.1K　　⟲ 45K　　♡ 189.1K　　⬆️

Donald J. Trump ✓ @realDonaldTrump · Apr 12, 2020
I am working hard to expose the corruption and dishonesty in the Lamestream Media. That part is easy, the hard part is WHY?

💬 77.3K　　⟲ 75K　　♡ 362K　　⬆️

Donald J. Trump ✓ @realDonaldTrump · Apr 14, 2020
GET RID OF BALLOT HARVESTING, IT IS RAMPANT WITH FRAUD. THE USA MUST HAVE VOTER I.D., THE ONLY WAY TO GET AN HONEST COUNT!

💬 41.7K　　⟲ 67.2K　　♡ 257K　　⬆️

Donald J. Trump ✓ @realDonaldTrump · Apr 17, 2020 ⚬⚬⚬
LIBERATE MICHIGAN!

💬 43.3K 🔁 50.2K ♡ 189.3K ↥

Donald J. Trump ✓ @realDonaldTrump · Apr 20, 2020 ⚬⚬⚬
In light of the attack from the Invisible Enemy, as well as the need to protect the jobs of our GREAT American Citizens, I will be signing an Executive Order to temporarily suspend immigration into the United States!

💬 69K 🔁 108.3K ♡ 370.4K ↥

Donald J. Trump ✓ @realDonaldTrump · Apr 22, 2020 ⚬⚬⚬
I have instructed the United States Navy to shoot down and destroy any and all Iranian gunboats if they harass our ships at sea.

💬 65.6K 🔁 103.5K ♡ 412.2K ↥

Donald J. Trump ✓ @realDonaldTrump · Apr 25, 2020 ⚬⚬⚬
What is the purpose of having White House News Conferences when the Lamestream Media asks nothing but hostile questions, & then refuses to report the truth or facts accurately. They get record ratings, & the American people get nothing but Fake News. Not worth the time & effort!

💬 92.8K 🔁 59.6K ♡ 218.8K ↥

Donald J. Trump ✓ @realDonaldTrump · Apr 26, 2020 ⚬⚬⚬
Happy Birthday to Melania, our great First Lady!

💬 48.9K 🔁 65.5K ♡ 535.3K ↥

Donald J. Trump ✓ @realDonaldTrump · Apr 27, 2020 ⚬⚬⚬
FAKE NEWS, THE ENEMY OF THE PEOPLE!

💬 69.6K 🔁 83.1K ♡ 365.2K ↥

Donald J. Trump ✓ @realDonaldTrump · Apr 27, 2020 ⚬⚬⚬
Why should the people and taxpayers of America be bailing out poorly run states (like Illinois, as example) and cities, in all cases Democrat run and managed, when most of the other states are not looking for bailout help? I am open to discussing anything, but just asking?

💬 73.5K 🔁 51.1K ♡ 196.1K ↥

Donald J. Trump ✓ @realDonaldTrump · Apr 29, 2020 ⚬⚬⚬
The only reason the U.S. has reported one million cases of CoronaVirus is that our Testing is sooo much better than any other country in the World. Other countries are way behind us in Testing, and therefore show far fewer cases!

💬 61.1K 🔁 54.9K ♡ 239.9K ↥

Donald J. Trump ✔ @realDonaldTrump · May 4, 2020

Mexico is sadly experiencing very big CoronaVirus problems, and now California, get this, doesn't want people coming over the Southern Border. A Classic! They are sooo lucky that I am their President. Border is very tight and the Wall is rapidly being built!

💬 36.1K   🔁 60.3K   ♡ 245.8K   ⬆️

Donald J. Trump ✔ @realDonaldTrump · May 11, 2020

OBAMAGATE makes Watergate look small time!

💬 40.7K   🔁 83.4K   ♡ 284.5K   ⬆️

Donald J. Trump ✔ @realDonaldTrump · May 12, 2020

Asian Americans are VERY angry at what China has done to our Country, and the World. Chinese Americans are the most angry of all. I don't blame them!

💬 31.6K   🔁 41.9K   ♡ 175.3K   ⬆️

Donald J. Trump ✔ @realDonaldTrump · May 14, 2020

Thank you to all of my great Keyboard Warriors. You are better, and far more brilliant, than anyone on Madison Avenue (Ad Agencies). There is nobody like you!

💬 43.1K   🔁 80.1K   ♡ 271.8K   ⬆️

Donald J. Trump ✔ @realDonaldTrump · May 18, 2020

REOPEN OUR COUNTRY!

💬 60K   🔁 116.5K   ♡ 494K   ⬆️

Donald J. Trump ✔ @realDonaldTrump · May 18, 2020

LOSER!

From **Donald J. Trump** ✔

💬 45.2K   🔁 35K   ♡ 124.7K   ⬆️

Donald J. Trump ✔ @realDonaldTrump · May 20, 2020   ०००
Congratulations to my daughter, Tiffany, on graduating from Georgetown
Law. Great student, great school. Just what I need is a lawyer in the family.
Proud of you Tiff!

💬 31.3K   🔁 48.2K   ♡ 386.1K   ⬆️

Donald J. Trump ✔ @realDonaldTrump · May 20, 2020   ०००
China is on a massive disinformation campaign because they are desperate
to have Sleepy Joe Biden win the presidential race so they can continue to
rip-off the United States, as they have done for decades, until I came along!

💬 44.6K   🔁 59.6K   ♡ 232.6K   ⬆️

Donald J. Trump ✔ @realDonaldTrump · May 21, 2020   ०००
96% Approval Rating in the Republican Party. Thank you!

💬 32.2K   🔁 36.1K   ♡ 234.8K   ⬆️

Donald J. Trump ✔ @realDonaldTrump · May 23, 2020   ०००
MAKE AMERICA GREAT AGAIN!

💬 48.7K   🔁 66.4K   ♡ 375.2K   ⬆️

Donald J. Trump ✔ @realDonaldTrump · May 24, 2020   ०००
The United States cannot have all Mail In Ballots. It will be the greatest
Rigged Election in history. People grab them from mailboxes, print
thousands of forgeries and "force" people to sign. Also, forge names. Some
absentee OK, when necessary. Trying to use Covid for this Scam!

💬 57.7K   🔁 61.8K   ♡ 187.2K   ⬆️

Donald J. Trump ✔ @realDonaldTrump · May 24, 2020   ०००
OBAMAGATE!

💬 55.7K   🔁 67.8K   ♡ 293.2K   ⬆️

Donald J. Trump ✔ @realDonaldTrump · May 26, 2020   ०००
.@Twitter is now interfering in the 2020 Presidential Election. They are saying
my statement on Mail-In Ballots, which will lead to massive corruption and
fraud, is incorrect, based on fact-checking by Fake News CNN and the
Amazon Washington Post....

💬 58.8K   🔁 73.5K   ♡ 205.2K   ⬆️

Donald J. Trump ✔ @realDonaldTrump · May 26, 2020   ०००
....Twitter is completely stifling FREE SPEECH, and I, as President, will not
allow it to happen!

💬 79.3K   🔁 70.7K   ♡ 191.7K   ⬆️

Donald J. Trump ✓ @realDonaldTrump · May 26, 2020   ⚬⚬⚬

The Failing @nytimes, winner of @PulitzerPrizes for its totally flawed coverage of the illegal Russia Witch Hunt, does its research as follows: Think of the absolute worst things you can say about Donald J. Trump, pretend there are sources, and just say it. RETURN THE PULITZERS!

💬 15.4K   ⟲ 19.1K   ♡ 67.4K   ⬆

Donald J. Trump ✓ @realDonaldTrump · May 27, 2020   ⚬⚬⚬

OBAMAGATE MAKES WATERGATE LOOK LIKE SMALL POTATOES!

💬 76.6K   ⟲ 69.1K   ♡ 256.3K   ⬆

Donald J. Trump ✓ @realDonaldTrump · May 27, 2020   ⚬⚬⚬

WARRANTLESS SURVEILLANCE OF AMERICANS IS WRONG!

💬 37.8K   ⟲ 58.3K   ♡ 246.2K   ⬆

Donald J. Trump ✓ @realDonaldTrump · May 27, 2020   ⚬⚬⚬

If the FISA Bill is passed tonight on the House floor, I will quickly VETO it. Our Country has just suffered through the greatest political crime in its history. The massive abuse of FISA was a big part of it!

💬 17.3K   ⟲ 38K   ♡ 147K   ⬆

Donald J. Trump ✓ @realDonaldTrump · May 27, 2020   ⚬⚬⚬

At my request, the FBI and the Department of Justice are already well into an investigation as to the very sad and tragic death in Minnesota of George Floyd....

💬 21.6K   ⟲ 51.2K   ♡ 227.7K   ⬆

Donald J. Trump ✓ @realDonaldTrump · May 27, 2020   ⚬⚬⚬

....I have asked for this investigation to be expedited and greatly appreciate all of the work done by local law enforcement. My heart goes out to George's family and friends. Justice will be served!

💬 9.3K   ⟲ 25.9K   ♡ 129K   ⬆

Donald J. Trump ✓ @realDonaldTrump · May 27, 2020   ⚬⚬⚬

Big Tech is doing everything in their very considerable power to CENSOR in advance of the 2020 Election. If that happens, we no longer have our freedom. I will never let it happen! They tried hard in 2016, and lost. Now they are going absolutely CRAZY. Stay Tuned!!!

💬 32.1K   ⟲ 45.9K   ♡ 163.1K   ⬆

Donald J. Trump ✓ @realDonaldTrump · May 28, 2020

We have just reached a very sad milestone with the coronavirus pandemic deaths reaching 100,000. To all of the families & friends of those who have passed, I want to extend my heartfelt sympathy & love for everything that these great people stood for & represent. God be with you!

💬 47.3K   🔁 35.7K   ♡ 173.1K   ⬆️

Donald J. Trump ✓ @realDonaldTrump · May 28, 2020

MAIL-IN VOTING WILL LEAD TO MASSIVE FRAUD AND ABUSE. IT WILL ALSO LEAD TO THE END OF OUR GREAT REPUBLICAN PARTY. WE CAN NEVER LET THIS TRAGEDY BEFALL OUR NATION. BIG MAIL-IN VICTORY IN TEXAS COURT TODAY. CONGRATS!!!

💬 59.4K   🔁 59.5K   ♡ 223.2K   ⬆️

Donald J. Trump ✓ @realDonaldTrump · May 29, 2020

This Tweet violated the Twitter Rules about glorifying violence. However, Twitter has determined that it may be in the public's interest for the Tweet to remain accessible. Learn more   **View**

💬   🔁   ♡   ⬆️

Donald J. Trump ✓ @realDonaldTrump · May 29, 2020

Twitter is doing nothing about all of the lies & propaganda being put out by China or the Radical Left Democrat Party. They have targeted Republicans, Conservatives & the President of the United States. Section 230 should be revoked by Congress. Until then, it will be regulated!

💬 56.5K   🔁 70.7K   ♡ 245.1K   ⬆️

Donald J. Trump ✓ @realDonaldTrump · May 30, 2020

These are "Organized Groups" that have nothing to do with George Floyd. Sad!

💬 39.8K   🔁 68.6K   ♡ 286.7K   ⬆️

Donald J. Trump ✓ @realDonaldTrump · May 30, 2020

It's ANTIFA and the Radical Left. Don't lay the blame on others!

💬 63K   🔁 91.3K   ♡ 330K   ⬆️

Donald J. Trump ✓ @realDonaldTrump · May 31, 2020

FAKE NEWS!

💬 131.6K   🔁 102.8K   ♡ 395.5K   ⬆️

Donald J. Trump ✔ @realDonaldTrump · Jun 2, 2020

Yesterday was a bad day for the Cuomo Brothers. New York was lost to the looters, thugs, Radical Left, and all others forms of Lowlife & Scum. The Governor refuses to accept my offer of a dominating National Guard. NYC was ripped to pieces. Likewise, Fredo's ratings are down 50%!

💬 45K   🔁 52.6K   ♡ 181.8K   ⬆️

Donald J. Trump ✔ @realDonaldTrump · Jun 2, 2020

NYC, CALL UP THE NATIONAL GUARD. The lowlifes and losers are ripping you apart. Act fast! Don't make the same horrible and deadly mistake you made with the Nursing Homes!!!

💬 30.9K   🔁 62.5K   ♡ 232.5K   ⬆️

Donald J. Trump ✔ @realDonaldTrump · Jun 2, 2020

SILENT MAJORITY!

💬 70.2K   🔁 93.8K   ♡ 421.2K   ⬆️

Donald J. Trump ✔ @realDonaldTrump · Jun 3, 2020

LAW & ORDER!

💬 66K   🔁 68.5K   ♡ 342.8K   ⬆️

Donald J. Trump ✔ @realDonaldTrump · Jun 3, 2020

If you watch Fake News @CNN or MSDNC, you would think that the killers, terrorists, arsonists, anarchists, thugs, hoodlums, looters, ANTIFA & others, would be the nicest, kindest most wonderful people in the Whole Wide World. No, they are what they are - very bad for our Country!

💬 43.6K   🔁 56.6K   ♡ 202.9K   ⬆️

Donald J. Trump ✔ @realDonaldTrump · Jun 4, 2020

MAKE AMERICA GREAT AGAIN!

💬 117.4K   🔁 110.4K   ♡ 515.6K   ⬆️

Donald J. Trump ✔ @realDonaldTrump · Jun 4, 2020

YOU DON'T BURN CHURCHES IN AMERICA!

💬 82.9K   🔁 119.3K   ♡ 548.3K   ⬆️

Donald J. Trump ✔ @realDonaldTrump · Jun 10, 2020

NASDAQ HITS ALL-TIME HIGH. Tremendous progress being made, way ahead of schedule. USA!

💬 18.8K   🔁 33.1K   ♡ 164.9K   ⬆️

Donald J. Trump ✔ @realDonaldTrump · Jun 11, 2020

THOSE THAT DENY THEIR HISTORY ARE DOOMED TO REPEAT IT!

💬 78.6K   🔁 102.8K   ♡ 396.7K   ⬆

Donald J. Trump ✔ @realDonaldTrump · Jun 14, 2020

Interesting how ANTIFA and other Far Left militant groups can take over a city without barely a wimpier from soft Do Nothing Democrat leadership, yet these same weak leaders become RADICAL when it comes to shutting down a state or city and its hard working, tax paying citizens!

💬 54.3K   🔁 66.3K   ♡ 242.9K   ⬆

Donald J. Trump ✔ @realDonaldTrump · Jun 14, 2020

THE SILENT MAJORITY IS STRONGER THAN EVER!!!

💬 89.5K   🔁 90.7K   ♡ 438.6K   ⬆

Donald J. Trump ✔ @realDonaldTrump · Jun 15, 2020

I've done more in less than 4 years than Biden's done in more than 40 years, including for Black America. Biden has been a part of every failed decision for decades. Bad Trade Deals, Endless Wars, you name it, he has shown a complete lack of leadership. He's weak & shot!!!

💬 55.1K   🔁 56.6K   ♡ 231.8K   ⬆

Donald J. Trump ✔ @realDonaldTrump · Jun 16, 2020

96% Approval Rating in the Republican Party. Thank you!

💬 66.1K   🔁 50.4K   ♡ 327K   ⬆

Donald J. Trump ✔ @realDonaldTrump · Jun 18, 2020

Do you get the impression that the Supreme Court doesn't like me?

💬 182K   🔁 103.2K   ♡ 323.4K   ⬆

Donald J. Trump ✔ @realDonaldTrump · Jun 18, 2020

As President of the United States, I am asking for a legal solution on DACA, not a political one, consistent with the rule of law. The Supreme Court is not willing to give us one, so now we have to start this process all over again.

💬 29.6K   🔁 34.3K   ♡ 127.6K   ⬆

Donald J. Trump ✔ @realDonaldTrump · Jun 18, 2020

First thing the anarchists did upon taking over Seattle was "BUILD A WALL". See, I was ahead of our times!

💬 37.7K   🔁 70.1K   ♡ 298.6K   ⬆

Donald J. Trump ✓ @realDonaldTrump · Jun 19, 2020   ⊙⊙⊙

Any protesters, anarchists, agitators, looters or lowlifes who are going to Oklahoma please understand, you will not be treated like you have been in New York, Seattle, or Minneapolis. It will be a much different scene!

💬 109.3K   ↻ 98.8K   ♡ 338.7K   ⬆

Donald J. Trump ✓ @realDonaldTrump · Jun 19, 2020   ⊙⊙⊙

Joe Biden's rally. ZERO enthusiasm!

💬 44.9K   ↻ 46.8K   ♡ 183.3K   ⬆

Donald J. Trump ✓ @realDonaldTrump · Jun 20, 2020   ⊙⊙⊙

THE SILENT MAJORITY IS STRONGER THAN EVER BEFORE! #MAGA

💬 75.7K   ↻ 69.5K   ♡ 274.6K   ⬆

Donald J. Trump ✔ @realDonaldTrump · Jun 22, 2020   ০০০

RIGGED 2020 ELECTION: MILLIONS OF MAIL-IN BALLOTS WILL BE PRINTED BY FOREIGN COUNTRIES, AND OTHERS. IT WILL BE THE SCANDAL OF OUR TIMES!

💬 111.3K   ↻ 127.2K   ♡ 289.1K   ⬆️

Donald J. Trump ✔ @realDonaldTrump · Jun 22, 2020   ০০০

Unlike the radical left, I will ALWAYS stand against socialism and with the people of Venezuela. My Admin has always stood on the side of FREEDOM and LIBERTY and against the oppressive Maduro regime! I would only meet with Maduro to discuss one thing: a peaceful exit from power!

💬 25.9K   ↻ 50.9K   ♡ 168.2K   ⬆️

Donald J. Trump ✔ @realDonaldTrump · Jun 22, 2020   ০০০

If people can go out and protest, riot, break into stores, and create all sorts of havoc, they can also go out and VOTE — and keep our Election Honest. With millions of mail-in ballots being sent out, who knows where they are going, and to whom?

💬 46.3K   ↻ 61.8K   ♡ 223.7K   ⬆️

Donald J. Trump ✔ @realDonaldTrump · Jun 23, 2020   ০০০

I have authorized the Federal Government to arrest anyone who vandalizes or destroys any monument, statue or other such Federal property in the U.S. with up to 10 years in prison, per the Veteran's Memorial Preservation Act, or such other laws that may be pertinent.....

💬 35.9K   ↻ 84.5K   ♡ 289K   ⬆️

Donald J. Trump ✔ @realDonaldTrump · Jun 23, 2020   ০০০

.....This action is taken effective immediately, but may also be used retroactively for destruction or vandalism already caused. There will be no exceptions!

💬 11.6K   ↻ 35.5K   ♡ 152.6K   ⬆️

Donald J. Trump ✔ @realDonaldTrump · Jun 23, 2020   ০০০

It is ashame that Congress doesn't do something about the lowlifes that burn the American Flag. It should be stopped, and now!

💬 60.2K   ↻ 50.5K   ♡ 230.9K   ⬆️

Donald J. Trump ✔ @realDonaldTrump · Jun 25, 2020   ০০০

Black Lives Matter leader states, "If U.S. doesn't give us what we want, then we will burn down this system and replace it". This is Treason, Sedition, Insurrection!

💬 58.6K   ↻ 81.1K   ♡ 253.2K   ⬆️

Donald J. Trump ✔ @realDonaldTrump · Jun 28, 2020

Since imposing a very powerful 10 year prison sentence on those that Vandalize Monuments, Statues etc., with many people being arrested all over our Country, the Vandalism has completely stopped. Thank you!

💬 36K   🔁 55.2K   ♡ 231.9K

Donald J. Trump ✔ @realDonaldTrump · Jun 28, 2020

THE VAST SILENT MAJORITY IS ALIVE AND WELL!!! We will win this Election big. Nobody wants a Low IQ person in charge of our Country, and Sleepy Joe is definitely a Low IQ person!

💬 99K   🔁 64.9K   ♡ 263.9K

Donald J. Trump ✔ @realDonaldTrump · Jul 6, 2020

SCHOOLS MUST OPEN IN THE FALL!!!

💬 85.7K   🔁 90.4K   ♡ 419.9K

Donald J. Trump ✔ @realDonaldTrump · Jul 10, 2020

President Trump Approval Rating in the Republican Party at 96%. Thank You!

💬 54.7K   🔁 42.1K   ♡ 250.2K

Donald J. Trump ✔ @realDonaldTrump · Jul 10, 2020

Too many Universities and School Systems are about Radical Left Indoctrination, not Education. Therefore, I am telling the Treasury Department to re-examine their Tax-Exempt Status...

💬 64.5K   🔁 95.6K   ♡ 289.9K

Donald J. Trump ✔ @realDonaldTrump · Jul 10, 2020

... and/or Funding, which will be taken away if this Propaganda or Act Against Public Policy continues. Our children must be Educated, not Indoctrinated!

💬 20.8K   🔁 36.7K   ♡ 148.4K

Donald J. Trump ✔ @realDonaldTrump · Jul 10, 2020

I LOVE @GoyaFoods!

💬 48.8K   🔁 63.7K   ♡ 279.3K

Donald J. Trump ✔ @realDonaldTrump · Jul 11, 2020

2016? HERE WE GO AGAIN!

💬 34K   🔁 44.7K   ♡ 268K

Donald J. Trump ✔ @realDonaldTrump · Jul 19, 2020

MAKE AMERICA GREAT AGAIN!

💬 114.1K   🔁 98.5K   ♡ 520.4K

Donald J. Trump ✔ @realDonaldTrump · Jul 20, 2020   ○○○

We are United in our effort to defeat the Invisible China Virus, and many people say that it is Patriotic to wear a face mask when you can't socially distance. There is nobody more Patriotic than me, your favorite President!

○ 148K   ⟲ 104.1K   ♡ 300.9K   ⬆

Donald J. Trump ✔ @realDonaldTrump · Jul 21, 2020   ○○○

Mail-In Voting, unless changed by the courts, will lead to the most CORRUPT ELECTION in our Nation's History! #RIGGEDELECTION

○ 63.7K   ⟲ 50K   ♡ 159.1K   ⬆

Donald J. Trump ✔ @realDonaldTrump · Jul 24, 2020   ○○○

So Obama and his team of lowlifes spied on my campaign, and got caught - Open and shut case! More papers released today which are devastating to them. Will they ever pay the price? The political Crime of the Century!

○ 61.7K   ⟲ 76.4K   ♡ 279.7K   ⬆

Donald J. Trump ✔ @realDonaldTrump · Jul 27, 2020   ○○○

So disgusting to watch Twitter's so-called "Trending", where sooo many trends are about me, and never a good one. They look for anything they can find, make it as bad as possible, and blow it up, trying to make it trend. Really ridiculous, illegal, and, of course, very unfair!

○ 175.4K   ⟲ 95.3K   ♡ 294.1K   ⬆

Donald J. Trump ✔ @realDonaldTrump · Jul 29, 2020   ○○○

Sleepy Joe Biden is just a Trojan Horse for the Radical Left Agenda. He will do whatever they want!

○ 38.6K   ⟲ 42.6K   ♡ 178.9K   ⬆

Donald J. Trump ✔ @realDonaldTrump · Jul 29, 2020

Germany pays Russia billions of dollars a year for Energy, and we are supposed to protect Germany from Russia. What's that all about? Also, Germany is very delinquent in their 2% fee to NATO. We are therefore moving some troops out of Germany!

💬 44.2K   🔁 49.8K   ♡ 180.5K   ⬆️

Donald J. Trump ✔ @realDonaldTrump · Jul 30, 2020

With Universal Mail-In Voting (not Absentee Voting, which is good), 2020 will be the most INACCURATE & FRAUDULENT Election in history. It will be a great embarrassment to the USA. Delay the Election until people can properly, securely and safely vote???

💬 183.9K   🔁 127.5K   ♡ 225.4K   ⬆️

Donald J. Trump ✔ @realDonaldTrump · Jul 30, 2020

Must know Election results on the night of the Election, not days, months, or even years later!

💬 34.8K   🔁 39.6K   ♡ 163.1K   ⬆️

Donald J. Trump ✔ @realDonaldTrump · Jul 30, 2020

We are going to WIN the 2020 Election, BIG! #MAGA

💬 79.7K   🔁 88.4K   ♡ 421.6K   ⬆️

Donald J. Trump ✔ @realDonaldTrump · Aug 3, 2020

FAKE NEWS IS THE ENEMY OF THE PEOPLE!

💬 83.3K   🔁 93.8K   ♡ 402.7K   ⬆️

Donald J. Trump ✔ @realDonaldTrump · Aug 3, 2020

OPEN THE SCHOOLS!!!

💬 121.2K   🔁 109.2K   ♡ 453.9K   ⬆️

Donald J. Trump ✔ @realDonaldTrump · Aug 4, 2020

I am deeply saddened by the tragic loss of eight Marines and one Sailor during a training exercise off the coast of California. Our prayers are with their families. I thank them for the brave service their loved ones gave to our Nation. #SemperFidelis

💬 13.4K   🔁 33K   ♡ 176.2K   ⬆️

Donald J. Trump ✔ @realDonaldTrump · Aug 5, 2020

There is TREMENDOUS Lawlessness in America's Liberal Cities. Would be so easy to stop but they have a clouded vision of what should be done. They are indoctrinated with a philosophy which will never work, a philosophy which would destroy America. Portland would be the norm!

💬 15.2K   🔁 26.9K   ♡ 96.5K   ⬆️

Donald J. Trump ✔ @realDonaldTrump · Aug 7, 2020   ⠇
I called the politicization of the China Virus by the Radical Left Democrats a Hoax, not the China Virus itself. Everybody knows this except for the Fake and very Corrupt Media!

💬 29.5K   ⟲ 37.2K   ♡ 139.4K   ⬆

Donald J. Trump ✔ @realDonaldTrump · Aug 9, 2020   ⠇

💬 32.5K   ⟲ 43.5K   ♡ 193.8K   ⬆

Donald J. Trump ✔ @realDonaldTrump · Aug 13, 2020   ⠇
HUGE breakthrough today! Historic Peace Agreement between our two GREAT friends, Israel and the United Arab Emirates!

💬 26.2K   ⟲ 73.4K   ♡ 306.6K   ⬆

Donald J. Trump ✔ @realDonaldTrump · Aug 14, 2020   ⠇
I promised YOU I would not take a dime of salary as your President. I donate the entire $400,000! It is my honor to give $100,000 to @NatlParkService to help repair and restore our GREAT National Monuments. So important to our American History! Thank You!!

💬 40.3K   ⟲ 68.3K   ♡ 250.5K   ⬆

Donald J. Trump ✔ @realDonaldTrump · Aug 19, 2020
IF YOU CAN PROTEST IN PERSON, YOU CAN VOTE IN PERSON!

💬 86.6K   🔁 148.7K   ♡ 569.5K   ⬆

Donald J. Trump ✔ @realDonaldTrump · Aug 19, 2020
Don't buy GOODYEAR TIRES - They announced a BAN ON MAGA HATS. Get better tires for far less! (This is what the Radical Left Democrats do. Two can play the same game, and we have to start playing it now!).

💬 129.7K   🔁 114.7K   ♡ 280.8K   ⬆

Donald J. Trump ✔ @realDonaldTrump · Aug 19, 2020
HE SPIED ON MY CAMPAIGN, AND GOT CAUGHT!

💬 100.7K   🔁 70.7K   ♡ 281.1K   ⬆

Donald J. Trump ✔ @realDonaldTrump · Aug 20, 2020
To get into the Democrat National Convention, you must have an ID card with a picture...Yet the Democrats refuse to do this when it come to your very important VOTE! Gee, I wonder WHY???

💬 52.8K   🔁 78.7K   ♡ 242.1K   ⬆

Donald J. Trump ✔ @realDonaldTrump · Aug 21, 2020
Robert, I Love You. Rest In Peace!

💬 54.9K   🔁 57.4K   ♡ 470.9K   ⬆

Donald J. Trump ✔ @realDonaldTrump · Aug 22, 2020
The Democrats took the word GOD out of the Pledge of Allegiance at the Democrat National Convention. At first I thought they made a mistake, but it wasn't. It was done on purpose. Remember Evangelical Christians, and ALL, this is where they are coming from-it's done. Vote Nov 3!

💬 100.3K   🔁 83.3K   ♡ 216.4K   ⬆

Donald J. Trump ✔ @realDonaldTrump · Aug 23, 2020

This Tweet violated the Twitter Rules about civic and election integrity. However, Twitter has determined that it may be in the public's interest for the Tweet to remain accessible. Learn more   **View**

💬   🔁   ♡   ⬆

Donald J. Trump ✔ @realDonaldTrump · Aug 25, 2020
80 Million Unsolicited Ballots are impossible for election centers to tabulate accurately. The Democrats know this better than anyone else. The fraud and abuse will be an embarrassment to our Country. Hopefully the Courts will stop this scam!

💬 17.6K   🔁 33.6K   ♡ 119.9K   ⬆

Donald J. Trump ✔ @realDonaldTrump · Aug 27, 2020   ⚬⚬⚬
The Ten Most Dangerous Cities in the U.S. are ALL run by Democrats, and this
has gone on for DECADES!

  💬 34.9K   ⟲ 67K   ♡ 269.9K   ⬆️

Donald J. Trump ✔ @realDonaldTrump · Sep 1, 2020   ⚬⚬⚬
People are tired of watching the highly political @NBA. Basketball ratings
are WAY down, and they won't be coming back. I hope football and baseball
are watching and learning because the same thing will be happening to
them. Stand tall for our Country and our Flag!!!

  💬 39K   ⟲ 57K   ♡ 202K   ⬆️

Donald J. Trump ✔ @realDonaldTrump · Sep 4, 2020   ⚬⚬⚬
Another great day for peace with Middle East – Muslim-majority Kosovo and
Israel have agreed to normalize ties and establish diplomatic relations. Well-
done! More Islamic and Arab nations will follow soon!

  💬 12.2K   ⟲ 40.7K   ♡ 164.8K   ⬆️

Donald J. Trump ✔ @realDonaldTrump · Sep 7, 2020   ⚬⚬⚬
10.6 Million Jobs Created In Just 4 Months, A Record!!!

  💬 41.8K   ⟲ 53.6K   ♡ 276.8K   ⬆️

Donald J. Trump ✔ @realDonaldTrump · Sep 7, 2020   ⚬⚬⚬
Just heard that Wacko John Bolton was talking of the fact that I discussed
"love letters from Kim Jong Un" as though I viewed them as just that.
Obviously, was just being sarcastic. Bolton was such a jerk!

  💬 23.5K   ⟲ 20.5K   ♡ 97.5K   ⬆️

Donald J. Trump ✔ @realDonaldTrump · Sep 9, 2020   ⚬⚬⚬
We will be substantially LOWERING Medicare Premiums and Prescription
Drug Prices, bringing them down to levels that were not thought possible!

  💬 30.6K   ⟲ 47.5K   ♡ 203.7K   ⬆️

Donald J. Trump ✔ @realDonaldTrump · Sep 10, 2020   ⚬⚬⚬
Sending out 80 MILLION BALLOTS to people who aren't even asking for a
Ballot is unfair and a total fraud in the making. Look at what's going on right
now!

  💬 20K   ⟲ 29.1K   ♡ 93.1K   ⬆️

Donald J. Trump ✔ @realDonaldTrump · Sep 11, 2020   ⚬⚬⚬
Another HISTORIC breakthrough today! Our two GREAT friends Israel and the
Kingdom of Bahrain agree to a Peace Deal – the second Arab country to
make peace with Israel in 30 days!

  💬 22.6K   ⟲ 71.5K   ♡ 292.4K   ⬆️

Donald J. Trump ✓ @realDonaldTrump · Sep 13, 2020
Just signed a new Executive Order to LOWER DRUG PRICES! My Most Favored Nation order will ensure that our Country gets the same low price Big Pharma gives to other countries. The days of global freeriding at America's expense are over...

💬 21.2K   🔁 45K   ♡ 171.1K   ⬆

Donald J. Trump ✓ @realDonaldTrump · Sep 13, 2020
...and prices are coming down FAST! Also just ended all rebates to middlemen, further reducing prices.

💬 5.8K   🔁 15.9K   ♡ 74.5K   ⬆

Donald J. Trump ✓ @realDonaldTrump · Sep 14, 2020
I do!

> 🪂 **Tim Kennedy** ✓ @TimKennedyMMA · Sep 13, 2020
> On my podcast with @joerogan he offered to moderate a debate between @JoeBiden and @realDonaldTrump It would be four hours with no live audience. Just the two candidates, cameras, and their vision of how to move this country forward. Who wants this? #debates #Election2020

💬 12.7K   🔁 64.5K   ♡ 282.2K   ⬆

Donald J. Trump ✓ @realDonaldTrump · Sep 14, 2020
According to press reports, Iran may be planning an assassination, or other attack, against the United States in retaliation for the killing of terrorist leader Soleimani, which was carried out for his planning a future attack, murdering U.S. Troops, and the death & suffering...

💬 22K   🔁 34.6K   ♡ 114K   ⬆

Donald J. Trump ✓ @realDonaldTrump · Sep 14, 2020
...caused over so many years. Any attack by Iran, in any form, against the United States will be met with an attack on Iran that will be 1,000 times greater in magnitude!

💬 11.5K   🔁 24.3K   ♡ 100K   ⬆

Donald J. Trump ✓ @realDonaldTrump · Sep 16, 2020
Vaccines are moving along fast and safely!

💬 33.7K   🔁 28.2K   ♡ 186.8K   ⬆

Donald J. Trump ✔ @realDonaldTrump · Sep 17, 2020   ⌄⌄⌄

Twitter makes sure that Trending on Twitter is anything bad, Fake or not, about President Donald Trump. So obvious what they are doing. Being studied now!

💬 42.2K   ⇄ 42K   ♡ 165.9K   ↥

Donald J. Trump ✔ @realDonaldTrump · Sep 22, 2020   ⌄⌄⌄

A few weeks ago, I BANNED efforts to indoctrinate government employees with divisive and harmful sex and race-based ideologies. Today, I've expanded that ban to people and companies that do business...

💬 12.6K   ⇄ 40.1K   ♡ 153.2K   ↥

Donald J. Trump ✔ @realDonaldTrump · Sep 22, 2020   ⌄⌄⌄

...with our Country, the United States Military, Government Contractors, and Grantees. Americans should be taught to take PRIDE in our Great Country, and if you don't, there's nothing in it for you!

💬 7.2K   ⇄ 22.3K   ♡ 102.8K   ↥

Donald J. Trump ✔ @realDonaldTrump · Sep 27, 2020   ⌄⌄⌄

I will be strongly demanding a Drug Test of Sleepy Joe Biden prior to, or after, the Debate on Tuesday night. Naturally, I will agree to take one also. His Debate performances have been record setting UNEVEN, to put it mildly. Only drugs could have caused this discrepancy???

💬 103.7K   ⇄ 71.5K   ♡ 237.8K   ↥

Donald J. Trump ✔ @realDonaldTrump · Sep 28, 2020   ⌄⌄⌄

FAKE NEWS!

💬 79.9K   ⇄ 48.2K   ♡ 239.6K   ↥

Donald J. Trump ✔ @realDonaldTrump · Sep 28, 2020   ⌄⌄⌄

The Ballots being returned to States cannot be accurately counted. Many things are already going very wrong!

⚠️ Learn how voting by mail is safe and secure

💬 36.2K   ⇄ 40.4K   ♡ 128.4K   ↥

Donald J. Trump ✔ @realDonaldTrump · Sep 28, 2020   ⌄⌄⌄

Joe Biden just announced that he will not agree to a Drug Test. Gee, I wonder why?

💬 97.3K   ⇄ 96.5K   ♡ 388.7K   ↥

Donald J. Trump ✔ @realDonaldTrump · Sep 29, 2020
Wow. Won't let Poll Watchers & Security into Philadelphia Voting Places. There is only one reason why. Corruption!!! Must have a fair Election.

💬 21.7K   ⟲ 36.3K   ♡ 120.6K   ⬆

Donald J. Trump ✔ @realDonaldTrump · Oct 1, 2020
I won the debate big, based on compilation of polls etc. Thank you!

💬 93.6K   ⟲ 53.5K   ♡ 319.1K   ⬆

Donald J. Trump ✔ @realDonaldTrump · Oct 1, 2020
Why would I allow the Debate Commission to change the rules for the second and third Debates when I easily won last time?

💬 86.8K   ⟲ 49.7K   ♡ 231.3K   ⬆

Donald J. Trump ✔ @realDonaldTrump · Oct 2, 2020
Tonight, @FLOTUS and I tested positive for COVID-19. We will begin our quarantine and recovery process immediately. We will get through this TOGETHER!

💬 550.7K   ⟲ 897.6K   ♡ 1.8M   ⬆

Donald J. Trump ✔ @realDonaldTrump · Oct 2, 2020
Going well, I think! Thank you to all. LOVE!!!

💬 175.2K   ⟲ 176.7K   ♡ 1.1M   ⬆

Donald J. Trump ✔ @realDonaldTrump · Oct 3, 2020
Doctors, Nurses and ALL at the GREAT Walter Reed Medical Center, and others from likewise incredible institutions who have joined them, are AMAZING!!!Tremendous progress has been made over the last 6 months in fighting this PLAGUE. With their help, I am feeling well!

💬 92.5K   ⟲ 113K   ♡ 619.3K   ⬆

Donald J. Trump ✔ @realDonaldTrump · Oct 3, 2020
OUR GREAT USA WANTS & NEEDS STIMULUS. WORK TOGETHER AND GET IT DONE. Thank you!

💬 61.6K   ⟲ 107.2K   ♡ 621.7K   ⬆

Donald J. Trump ✔ @realDonaldTrump · Oct 4, 2020
I really appreciate all of the fans and supporters outside of the hospital. The fact is, they really love our Country and are seeing how we are MAKING IT GREATER THAN EVER BEFORE!

💬 71.1K   ⟲ 94.2K   ♡ 570.4K   ⬆

Donald J. Trump ✔ @realDonaldTrump · Oct 5, 2020

STOCK MARKET HIGHS. VOTE!

💬 12.6K   🔁 41.2K   ♡ 241.7K   ↑

Donald J. Trump ✔ @realDonaldTrump · Oct 5, 2020

STRONGEST EVER MILITARY. VOTE!

💬 9.4K   🔁 40.8K   ♡ 238.9K   ↑

Donald J. Trump ✔ @realDonaldTrump · Oct 5, 2020

LAW & ORDER. VOTE!

💬 11K   🔁 42.7K   ♡ 223.9K   ↑

Donald J. Trump ✔ @realDonaldTrump · Oct 5, 2020

RELIGIOUS LIBERTY. VOTE!

💬 12.8K   🔁 43.4K   ♡ 237.1K   ↑

Donald J. Trump ✔ @realDonaldTrump · Oct 5, 2020

BIGGEST TAX CUT EVER, AND ANOTHER ONE COMING. VOTE!

💬 15.9K   🔁 41.6K   ♡ 217.3K   ↑

Donald J. Trump ✔ @realDonaldTrump · Oct 5, 2020

401(K). VOTE!

💬 9.6K   🔁 35.2K   ♡ 214.5K   ↑

Donald J. Trump ✔ @realDonaldTrump · Oct 5, 2020

BEST V.A. EVER. 91% APPROVAL RATING. VOTE!

💬 8K   🔁 33.5K   ♡ 184.9K   ↑

Donald J. Trump ✔ @realDonaldTrump · Oct 5, 2020

SPACE FORCE. VOTE!

💬 26.9K   🔁 56.6K   ♡ 300.8K   ↑

Donald J. Trump ✔ @realDonaldTrump · Oct 5, 2020

MASSIVE REGULATION CUTS. VOTE!

💬 8K   🔁 34.3K   ♡ 188.4K   ↑

Donald J. Trump ✔ @realDonaldTrump · Oct 5, 2020

PRO LIFE! VOTE!

💬 47.8K   🔁 96.3K   ♡ 498.5K   ↑

Donald J. Trump ✔ @realDonaldTrump · Oct 5, 2020

BETTER & CHEAPER HEALTHCARE. VOTE!

💬 19.7K   🔁 40.4K   ♡ 215.9K   ↑

Donald J. Trump ✔ @realDonaldTrump · Oct 5, 2020
PROTECT PREEXISTING CONDITIONS. VOTE!

💬 31.2K   🔁 47.8K   ♡ 233.9K   ⬆️

Donald J. Trump ✔ @realDonaldTrump · Oct 5, 2020
FIGHT THE CORRUPT FAKE NEWS MEDIA. VOTE!

💬 28.8K   🔁 67.5K   ♡ 364.6K   ⬆️

Donald J. Trump ✔ @realDonaldTrump · Oct 5, 2020
SAVE OUR SECOND AMENDMENT. VOTE!

💬 18.9K   🔁 57.8K   ♡ 302.6K   ⬆️

Donald J. Trump ✔ @realDonaldTrump · Oct 5, 2020
PEACE THROUGH STRENGTH (BRING OUR SOLDIERS HOME). VOTE!

💬 25.7K   🔁 48.6K   ♡ 240.3K   ⬆️

Donald J. Trump ✔ @realDonaldTrump · Oct 5, 2020
I will be leaving the great Walter Reed Medical Center today at 6:30 P.M.
Feeling really good! Don't be afraid of Covid. Don't let it dominate your life.
We have developed, under the Trump Administration, some really great
drugs & knowledge. I feel better than I did 20 years ago!

💬 188.4K   🔁 275K   ♡ 566.9K   ⬆️

Donald J. Trump ✔ @realDonaldTrump · Oct 6, 2020
FEELING GREAT!

💬 70.5K   🔁 96.5K   ♡ 588.9K   ⬆️

Donald J. Trump ✔ @realDonaldTrump · Oct 6, 2020
Wear your mask in the "beauty" parlor, Nancy!

> 🔵 **Gregg Jarrett** ✔ @GreggJarrett · Oct 3, 2020
> Pelosi: Trump's behavior was a 'brazen invitation' for coronavirus infection
> gjarr.it/36v46Kf

💬 29.6K   🔁 50.6K   ♡ 205.3K   ⬆️

Donald J. Trump ✔ @realDonaldTrump · Oct 7, 2020
THE FAKE NEWS MEDIA IS THE REAL OPPOSITION PARTY!

💬 55K   🔁 83.3K   ♡ 418.7K   ⬆️

Donald J. Trump ✔ @realDonaldTrump · Oct 7, 2020
Mike Pence is doing GREAT! She is a gaffe machine.

💬 47.5K   🔁 62.3K   ♡ 410.1K   ⬆️

Donald J. Trump ✔ @realDonaldTrump · Oct 7, 2020

Mike Pence WON BIG!

💬 99.3K   🔁 94.2K   ♡ 603.7K   ⬆

Donald J. Trump ✔ @realDonaldTrump · Oct 8, 2020

If a Republican LIED like Biden and Harris do, constantly, the Lamestream Media would be calling them out at a level never recorded before. For one year they called for No Fracking and big Tax Increases. Now they each say opposite. Fake News is working overtime!

💬 32.8K   🔁 47.9K   ♡ 187.3K   ⬆

Donald J. Trump ✔ @realDonaldTrump · Oct 12, 2020

California is going to hell. Vote Trump!

💬 65K   🔁 119.1K   ♡ 456K   ⬆

Donald J. Trump ✔ @realDonaldTrump · Oct 13, 2020

💬 70.7K   🔁 195.3K   ♡ 608.2K   ⬆

Donald J. Trump ✔ @realDonaldTrump · Oct 15, 2020   ₀₀₀

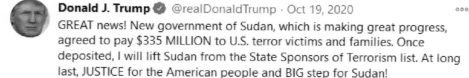

💬 6.5K   ⟲ 31.4K   ♡ 160.8K   ↑

Donald J. Trump ✔ @realDonaldTrump · Oct 17, 2020   ₀₀₀
GIANT RED WAVE COMING!

💬 59.4K   ⟲ 89.5K   ♡ 423K   ↑

Donald J. Trump ✔ @realDonaldTrump · Oct 18, 2020   ₀₀₀
Hunter Biden's laptop is a disaster for the entire Biden family, but especially
for his father, Joe. It is now a proven fact, and cannot be denied, that all of
that info is the REAL DEAL. That makes it impossible for "50%, or 10%" Joe,
to ever assume the office of the President!

💬 45.7K   ⟲ 85.1K   ♡ 259.7K   ↑

Donald J. Trump ✔ @realDonaldTrump · Oct 18, 2020   ₀₀₀
Big problems and discrepancies with Mail In Ballots all over the USA. Must
have final total on November 3rd.

⚠ Learn how voting by mail is safe and secure

💬   ⟲   ♡   ↑

Donald J. Trump ✔ @realDonaldTrump · Oct 18, 2020   ₀₀₀
Corrupt politician Joe Biden makes Crooked Hillary look like an amateur!

💬 47.3K   ⟲ 66.2K   ♡ 307K   ↑

Donald J. Trump ✔ @realDonaldTrump · Oct 19, 2020   ₀₀₀
GREAT news! New government of Sudan, which is making great progress,
agreed to pay $335 MILLION to U.S. terror victims and families. Once
deposited, I will lift Sudan from the State Sponsors of Terrorism list. At long
last, JUSTICE for the American people and BIG step for Sudan!

💬 19.6K   ⟲ 70.5K   ♡ 241.5K   ↑

Donald J. Trump ✔ @realDonaldTrump · Oct 19, 2020

...P.S. Tony should stop wearing the Washington Nationals' Mask for two reasons. Number one, it is not up to the high standards that he should be exposing. Number two, it keeps reminding me that Tony threw out perhaps the worst first pitch in the history of Baseball!

💬 22.9K   ↻ 22.2K   ♡ 82.9K   ⬆️

Donald J. Trump ✔ @realDonaldTrump · Oct 22, 2020

Obama is campaigning for us. Every time he speaks, people come over to our side. He didn't even want to endorse Sleepy Joe. Did so long after primaries were over!

💬 24.9K   ↻ 38.1K   ♡ 194.4K   ⬆️

Donald J. Trump ✔ @realDonaldTrump · Oct 22, 2020

Biden wants to Pack the Court with Radical Left crazies. He doesn't even want to make a list to explain who they are. Can't let this happen!

💬 18.3K   ↻ 30.1K   ♡ 146K   ⬆️

Donald J. Trump ✔ @realDonaldTrump · Oct 24, 2020

JUST VOTED. A great honor!

💬 31.6K   ↻ 45.8K   ♡ 372.4K   ⬆️

Donald J. Trump ✔ @realDonaldTrump · Oct 25, 2020

Congratulations to Armenian Prime Minister Nikol Pashinyan and Azerbaijani President Ilham Aliyev, who just agreed to adhere to a cease fire effective at midnight. Many lives will be saved. Proud of my team @SecPompeo & Steve Biegun & @WHNSC for getting the deal done!

💬 13.5K   ↻ 43.6K   ♡ 174.4K   ⬆️

Donald J. Trump ✔ @realDonaldTrump · Oct 26, 2020

Joe Biden called me George yesterday. Couldn't remember my name. Got some help from the anchor to get him through the interview. The Fake News Cartel is working overtime to cover it up!

💬 31K   ↻ 61.8K   ♡ 264.9K   ⬆️

Donald J. Trump ✔ @realDonaldTrump · Oct 26, 2020

The Fake News Media is riding COVID, COVID, COVID, all the way to the Election. Losers!

💬 56.7K   ↻ 66.3K   ♡ 313.8K   ⬆️

Donald J. Trump ✔ @realDonaldTrump · Oct 28, 2020 ○○○

From **The Election Wizard**

💬 33.1K   ⟲ 69.5K   ♡ 260.4K   ⬆

 Donald J. Trump ✔ @realDonaldTrump · Oct 28, 2020 ○○○
Why isn't Twitter trending Biden corruption? It's the biggest, and most credible, story anywhere in the world. Fake Trending!!!

💬 53.3K   ⟲ 78.7K   ♡ 326.2K   ⬆

 Donald J. Trump ✔ @realDonaldTrump · Nov 1, 2020 ○○○
Joe Biden is the candidate of rioters, looters, arsonists, gun-grabbers, flag-burners, Marxists, lobbyists, and special interests. I am the candidate of farmers, factory workers, police officers, and hard-working, law-abiding patriots of every race, religion and creed! #MAGA

💬 25.7K   ⟲ 53.8K   ♡ 195K   ⬆

Donald J. Trump ✔ @realDonaldTrump · Nov 2, 2020

Just signed an order to establish the 1776 Commission. We will stop the radical indoctrination of our students, and restore PATRIOTIC EDUCATION to our schools!

💬 23.5K   🔁 69.1K   ♡ 256.2K   ⬆️

Donald J. Trump ✔ @realDonaldTrump · Nov 3, 2020

To all of our supporters: thank you from the bottom of my heart. You have been there from the beginning, and I will never let you down. Your hopes are my hopes, your dreams are my dreams, and your future is what I am fighting for every single day! Vote.DonaldJTrump.com

💬 24.1K   🔁 71.2K   ♡ 298.6K   ⬆️

Donald J. Trump ✔ @realDonaldTrump · Nov 3, 2020

WE ARE LOOKING REALLY GOOD ALL OVER THE COUNTRY. THANK YOU!

💬 67.2K   🔁 128.4K   ♡ 926.7K   ⬆️

Donald J. Trump ✔ @realDonaldTrump · Nov 4, 2020

I will be making a statement tonight. A big WIN!

💬 107.5K   🔁 172.6K   ♡ 897.8K   ⬆️

Donald J. Trump ✔ @realDonaldTrump · Nov 4, 2020

We are up BIG, but they are trying to STEAL the Election. We will never let them do it. Votes cannot be cast after the Polls are closed!

⚠️ Learn about US 2020 election security efforts

💬   🔁   ♡   ⬆️

Donald J. Trump ✔ @realDonaldTrump · Nov 4, 2020

How come every time they count Mail-In ballot dumps they are so devastating in their percentage and power of destruction?

💬 105.3K   🔁 131.5K   ♡ 535.9K   ⬆️

Donald J. Trump ✔ @realDonaldTrump · Nov 4, 2020

They are finding Biden votes all over the place — in Pennsylvania, Wisconsin, and Michigan. So bad for our Country!

💬 176K   🔁 195.4K   ♡ 607.7K   ⬆

Donald J. Trump ✔ @realDonaldTrump · Nov 4, 2020

Our lawyers have asked for "meaningful access", but what good does that do? The damage has already been done to the integrity of our system, and to the Presidential Election itself. This is what should be discussed!

💬 114.8K   🔁 112.9K   ♡ 515.1K   ⬆

Donald J. Trump ✔ @realDonaldTrump · Nov 5, 2020

STOP THE COUNT!

💬 347.3K   🔁 438.3K   ♡ 729.1K   ⬆

Donald J. Trump ✔ @realDonaldTrump · Nov 6, 2020

I easily WIN the Presidency of the United States with LEGAL VOTES CAST. The OBSERVERS were not allowed, in any way, shape, or form, to do their job and therefore, votes accepted during this period must be determined to be ILLEGAL VOTES. U.S. Supreme Court should decide!

(!) Learn about US 2020 election security efforts

💬   🔁   ♡   ⬆

Donald J. Trump ✔ @realDonaldTrump · Nov 6, 2020

Twitter is out of control, made possible through the government gift of Section 230!

💬 121.2K   🔁 109.2K   ♡ 479.9K   ⬆

Donald J. Trump ✔ @realDonaldTrump · Nov 6, 2020

Where are the missing military ballots in Georgia? What happened to them?

💬 156.7K   🔁 148.1K   ♡ 631.1K   ⬆

Donald J. Trump ✔ @realDonaldTrump · Nov 6, 2020

Joe Biden should not wrongfully claim the office of the President. I could make that claim also. Legal proceedings are just now beginning!

💬 153K   🔁 163.3K   ♡ 655.2K   ⬆

Donald J. Trump ✔ @realDonaldTrump · Nov 6, 2020

I had such a big lead in all of these states late into election night, only to see the leads miraculously disappear as the days went by. Perhaps these leads will return as our legal proceedings move forward!

💬 180.4K   🔁 143.9K   ♡ 560.4K   ⬆

Donald J. Trump ✔ @realDonaldTrump · Nov 7, 2020   ⦁⦁⦁
I WON THIS ELECTION, BY A LOT!

⚠ Official sources may not have called the race when this was Tweeted

💬 956.4K   🔁 877.8K   ♡ 1.1M   ⬆

Donald J. Trump ✔ @realDonaldTrump · Nov 7, 2020   ⦁⦁⦁
THE OBSERVERS WERE NOT ALLOWED INTO THE COUNTING ROOMS. I
WON THE ELECTION, GOT 71,000,000 LEGAL VOTES. BAD THINGS
HAPPENED WHICH OUR OBSERVERS WERE NOT ALLOWED TO SEE. NEVER
HAPPENED BEFORE. MILLIONS OF MAIL-IN BALLOTS WERE SENT TO PEOPLE
WHO NEVER ASKED FOR THEM!

⚠ This claim about election fraud is disputed

💬 285.8K   🔁 255.5K   ♡ 664.2K   ⬆

Donald J. Trump ✔ @realDonaldTrump · Nov 7, 2020   ⦁⦁⦁
71,000,000 Legal Votes. The most EVER for a sitting President!

💬 428.4K   🔁 241.5K   ♡ 952.8K   ⬆

Donald J. Trump ✔ @realDonaldTrump · Nov 8, 2020   ⦁⦁⦁
Since when does the Lamestream Media call who our next president will be?
We have all learned a lot in the last two weeks!

💬 170K   🔁 151.5K   ♡ 668.8K   ⬆

Donald J. Trump ✔ @realDonaldTrump · Nov 9, 2020   ⦁⦁⦁
STOCK MARKET UP BIG, VACCINE COMING SOON. REPORT 90% EFFECTIVE.
SUCH GREAT NEWS!

💬 119.6K   🔁 119.7K   ♡ 700.6K   ⬆

Donald J. Trump ✔ @realDonaldTrump · Nov 9, 2020   ⦁⦁⦁
Pennsylvania prevented us from watching much of the Ballot count.
Unthinkable and illegal in this country.

⚠ This claim about election fraud is disputed

💬 51.4K   🔁 90.7K   ♡ 462.9K   ⬆

Donald J. Trump ✔ @realDonaldTrump · Nov 9, 2020   ⦁⦁⦁
Georgia will be a big presidential win, as it was the night of the Election!

💬 77.7K   🔁 107.5K   ♡ 617.8K   ⬆

Donald J. Trump ✔ @realDonaldTrump · Nov 9, 2020

As I have long said, @Pfizer and the others would only announce a Vaccine after the Election, because they didn't have the courage to do it before. Likewise, the @US_FDA should have announced it earlier, not for political purposes, but for saving lives!

💬 27.8K   🔁 64.9K   ♡ 281.7K   ⬆️

Donald J. Trump ✔ @realDonaldTrump · Nov 10, 2020

WE WILL WIN!

💬 223K   🔁 248.2K   ♡ 998.6K   ⬆️

Donald J. Trump ✔ @realDonaldTrump · Nov 10, 2020

BALLOT COUNTING ABUSE!

(!) This claim about election fraud is disputed

💬 58.1K   🔁 91.2K   ♡ 508.4K   ⬆️

Donald J. Trump ✔ @realDonaldTrump · Nov 10, 2020

People will not accept this Rigged Election!

(!) This claim about election fraud is disputed

> **Scott Adams** ✔ @ScottAdamsSays · Nov 10, 2020
>
> You are being brainwashed to accept the results of the election as fair. You will be told that only bad people are skeptical in this situation, and that you will be held to account for doubting.

💬 33.6K   🔁 57.3K   ♡ 245.5K   ⬆️

Donald J. Trump ✔ @realDonaldTrump · Nov 12, 2020

"REPORT: DOMINION DELETED 2.7 MILLION TRUMP VOTES NATIONWIDE. DATA ANALYSIS FINDS 221,000 PENNSYLVANIA VOTES SWITCHED FROM PRESIDENT TRUMP TO BIDEN. 941,000 TRUMP VOTES DELETED. STATES USING DOMINION VOTING SYSTEMS SWITCHED 435,000 VOTES FROM TRUMP TO BIDEN." @ChanelRion @OANN

(!) This claim about election fraud is disputed

💬 170.9K   🔁 243.8K   ♡ 600.6K   ⬆️

Donald J. Trump ✔ @realDonaldTrump · Nov 13, 2020

Heartwarming to see all of the tremendous support out there, especially the organic Rallies that are springing up all over the Country, including a big one on Saturday in D.C. I may even try to stop by and say hello. This Election was Rigged, from Dominion all the way up & down!

⚠ This claim about election fraud is disputed

💬 68.5K   🔁 93.4K   ♡ 391.5K   ⬆

Donald J. Trump ✔ @realDonaldTrump · Nov 14, 2020

Congress must now do a Covid Relief Bill. Needs Democrats support. Make it big and focused. Get it done!

💬 26.9K   🔁 52.9K   ♡ 306.2K   ⬆

Donald J. Trump ✔ @realDonaldTrump · Nov 14, 2020

There is tremendous evidence of wide spread voter fraud in that there is irrefutable proof that our Republican poll watchers and observers were not allowed to be present in poll counting rooms. Michigan, Pennsylvania, Georgia and others. Unconstitutional!

⚠ This claim about election fraud is disputed

💬 64.5K   🔁 80.8K   ♡ 322.6K   ⬆

Donald J. Trump ✔ @realDonaldTrump · Nov 14, 2020

I look forward to Mayor Giuliani spearheading the legal effort to defend OUR RIGHT to FREE and FAIR ELECTIONS! Rudy Giuliani, Joseph diGenova, Victoria Toensing, Sidney Powell, and Jenna Ellis, a truly great team, added to our other wonderful lawyers and representatives!

💬 48.4K   🔁 75.9K   ♡ 319.1K   ⬆

Donald J. Trump ✔ @realDonaldTrump · Nov 14, 2020

ANTIFA SCUM ran for the hills today when they tried attacking the people at the Trump Rally, because those people aggressively fought back. Antifa waited until tonight, when 99% were gone, to attack innocent #MAGA People. DC Police, get going — do your job and don't hold back!!!

💬 37.2K   🔁 83.6K   ♡ 329.6K   ⬆

Donald J. Trump ✔ @realDonaldTrump · Nov 15, 2020

All of the mechanical "glitches" that took place on Election Night were really THEM getting caught trying to steal votes. They succeeded plenty, however, without getting caught. Mail-in elections are a sick joke!

⚠ This claim about election fraud is disputed

💬 27.8K   🔁 57.9K   ♡ 259K   ⬆

Donald J. Trump ✔ @realDonaldTrump · Nov 15, 2020   ⦁⦁⦁
RIGGED ELECTION. WE WILL WIN!

(!) This claim about election fraud is disputed

💬 82K   ⟲ 115.3K   ♡ 588.9K   ⬆

Donald J. Trump ✔ @realDonaldTrump · Nov 15, 2020   ⦁⦁⦁
He only won in the eyes of the FAKE NEWS MEDIA. I concede NOTHING! We
have a long way to go. This was a RIGGED ELECTION!

(!) This claim about election fraud is disputed

💬 123.5K   ⟲ 153.8K   ♡ 555.7K   ⬆

Donald J. Trump ✔ @realDonaldTrump · Nov 15, 2020   ⦁⦁⦁
I WON THE ELECTION!

(!) Election officials have certified Joe Biden as the winner of the U.S.
       Presidential election

💬 261.8K   ⟲ 323.4K   ♡ 702.2K   ⬆

Donald J. Trump ✔ @realDonaldTrump · Nov 16, 2020   ⦁⦁⦁
Another Vaccine just announced. This time by Moderna, 95% effective. For
those great "historians", please remember that these great discoveries, which
will end the China Plague, all took place on my watch!

💬 76.6K   ⟲ 67.4K   ♡ 309.5K   ⬆

Donald J. Trump ✔ @realDonaldTrump · Nov 17, 2020   ⦁⦁⦁
I have reversed the ridiculous decision to cancel Wreaths Across America at
Arlington National Cemetery. It will now go on!

💬 38.4K   ⟲ 83.8K   ♡ 465.1K   ⬆

Donald J. Trump ✔ @realDonaldTrump · Nov 17, 2020   ⦁⦁⦁
Wow! Michigan just refused to certify the election results! Having courage is
a beautiful thing. The USA stands proud!

💬 71.6K   ⟲ 95.6K   ♡ 498.1K   ⬆

Donald J. Trump ✔ @realDonaldTrump · Nov 19, 2020   ooo

Look at this in Michigan! A day AFTER the election, Biden receives a dump of 134,886 votes at 6:31AM!

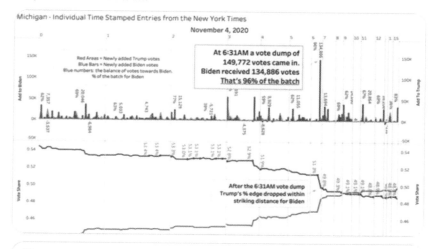

Michigan - Individual Time Stamped Entries from the New York Times

November 4, 2020

At 6:31AM a vote dump of 149,772 votes came in. Biden received 134,886 votes. That's 96% of the batch

After the 6:31AM vote dump Trump's % edge dropped within striking distance for Biden

---

Donald J. Trump ✔ @realDonaldTrump · Nov 18, 2020

Look at this in Wisconsin! A day AFTER the election, Biden receives a dump of 143,379 votes at 3:42AM, when they learned he was losing badly. This is unbelievable!

   💬 56.7K   🔁 76.5K   ♡ 214.7K   ⬆

Donald J. Trump ✔ @realDonaldTrump · Nov 21, 2020   ooo

The Media is just as corrupt as the Election itself!

   💬 85.4K   🔁 112.1K   ♡ 595.6K   ⬆

Donald J. Trump ✔ @realDonaldTrump · Nov 22, 2020   ooo

In certain swing states, there were more votes than people who voted, and in big numbers. Does that not really matter? Stopping Poll Watchers, voting for unsuspecting people, fake ballots and so much more. Such egregious conduct. We will win!

   ⚠   This claim about election fraud is disputed

   💬 78.5K   🔁 83.5K   ♡ 370.6K   ⬆

Donald J. Trump ✔ @realDonaldTrump · Nov 24, 2020   ooo

AMERICA FIRST!!!

   💬 60.9K   🔁 89.2K   ♡ 538.3K   ⬆

Donald J. Trump ✔ @realDonaldTrump · Nov 25, 2020

It is my Great Honor to announce that General Michael T. Flynn has been granted a Full Pardon. Congratulations to @GenFlynn and his wonderful family, I know you will now have a truly fantastic Thanksgiving!

💬 85.9K   🔁 130.2K   ♡ 461.7K   ⬆️

Donald J. Trump ✔ @realDonaldTrump · Nov 26, 2020

Just saw the vote tabulations. There is NO WAY Biden got 80,000,000 votes!!! This was a 100% RIGGED ELECTION.

⚠️ This claim about election fraud is disputed

💬 110.5K   🔁 126K   ♡ 483.8K   ⬆️

Donald J. Trump ✔ @realDonaldTrump · Nov 28, 2020

So much credit to all of the brave men and women in state houses who are defending our great Constitution. Thank you!

💬 29.5K   🔁 71.7K   ♡ 430.3K   ⬆️

Donald J. Trump ✔ @realDonaldTrump · Dec 4, 2020

The only thing more RIGGED than the 2020 Presidential Election is the FAKE NEWS SUPPRESSED MEDIA. No matter how big or important the story, if it is even slightly positive for "us", or negative for "them", it will not be reported!

⚠️ This claim about election fraud is disputed

💬 29.2K   🔁 65.6K   ♡ 247.9K   ⬆️

Donald J. Trump ✔ @realDonaldTrump · Dec 4, 2020

STOCK MARKET REACHES NEW ALL-TIME HIGH!

💬 37.5K   🔁 40.7K   ♡ 278.2K   ⬆️

Donald J. Trump ✔ @realDonaldTrump · Dec 7, 2020

The Republican Governor of Georgia refuses to do signature verification, which would give us an easy win. What's wrong with this guy? What is he hiding?

⚠️ This claim about election fraud is disputed

💬 57.4K   🔁 78.8K   ♡ 307.5K   ⬆️

Donald J. Trump ✔ @realDonaldTrump · Dec 8, 2020

NASDAQ and S&P close at all-time highs. Congratulations!

💬 42.4K   🔁 34.6K   ♡ 239.1K   ⬆️

Donald J. Trump ✔ @realDonaldTrump · Dec 9, 2020

Wow! At least 17 States have joined Texas in the extraordinary case against the greatest Election Fraud in the history of the United States. Thank you!

(!) This claim about election fraud is disputed

💬 44.5K   🔁 89K   ♡ 361.5K   ⬆

Donald J. Trump ✔ @realDonaldTrump · Dec 10, 2020

Another HISTORIC breakthrough today! Our two GREAT friends Israel and the Kingdom of Morocco have agreed to full diplomatic relations – a massive breakthrough for peace in the Middle East!

💬 14.1K   🔁 65.6K   ♡ 294K   ⬆

Donald J. Trump ✔ @realDonaldTrump · Dec 10, 2020

19 states are fighting for us, almost unheard of support!

💬 45K   🔁 68.2K   ♡ 403.2K   ⬆

Donald J. Trump ✔ @realDonaldTrump · Dec 11, 2020

I just want to stop the world from killing itself!

💬 96.5K   🔁 134.2K   ♡ 592.7K   ⬆

Donald J. Trump ✔ @realDonaldTrump · Dec 11, 2020

The Supreme Court really let us down. No Wisdom, No Courage!

💬 90.2K   🔁 73.2K   ♡ 346.3K   ⬆

Donald J. Trump ✔ @realDonaldTrump · Dec 12, 2020

I WON THE ELECTION IN A LANDSLIDE, but remember, I only think in terms of legal votes, not all of the fake voters and fraud that miraculously floated in from everywhere! What a disgrace!

(!) This claim about election fraud is disputed

Donald J. Trump ✔ @realDonaldTrump · Dec 12, 2020

WE HAVE JUST BEGUN TO FIGHT!!!

💬 106.3K   🔁 132.1K   ♡ 569.7K   ⬆

Donald J. Trump ✔ @realDonaldTrump · Dec 12, 2020

The Supreme Court had ZERO interest in the merits of the greatest voter fraud ever perpetrated on the United States of America. All they were interested in is "standing", which makes it very difficult for the President to present a case on the merits. 75,000,000 votes!

(!) This claim about election fraud is disputed

💬 69.4K   🔁 68.8K   ♡ 267.8K   ⬆

Donald J. Trump ✓ @realDonaldTrump · Dec 13, 2020

MOST CORRUPT ELECTION IN U.S. HISTORY!

(!) This claim about election fraud is disputed

💬 95.5K   ↻ 109.6K   ♡ 539.8K   ⬆️

Donald J. Trump ✓ @realDonaldTrump · Dec 13, 2020

Vaccines are shipped and on their way, FIVE YEARS AHEAD OF SCHEDULE. Get well USA. Get well WORLD. We love you all!

💬 41.7K   ↻ 55.2K   ♡ 348.1K   ⬆️

Donald J. Trump ✓ @realDonaldTrump · Dec 15, 2020

Tremendous evidence pouring in on voter fraud. There has never been anything like this in our Country!

(!) This claim about election fraud is disputed

💬 99.1K   ↻ 98.1K   ♡ 415.2K   ⬆️

Donald J. Trump ✓ @realDonaldTrump · Dec 15, 2020

Tremendous problems being found with voting machines. They are so far off it is ridiculous. Able to take a landslide victory and reduce it to a tight loss. This is not what the USA is all about. Law enforcement shielding machines. DO NOT TAMPER, a crime. Much more to come!

(!) This claim about election fraud is disputed

💬 31.3K   ↻ 67.8K   ♡ 268.6K   ⬆️

Donald J. Trump ✓ @realDonaldTrump · Dec 15, 2020

Poll: 92% of Republican Voters think the election was rigged!

💬 83.8K   ↻ 84.7K   ♡ 460.6K   ⬆️

Donald J. Trump ✓ @realDonaldTrump · Dec 17, 2020

I am very disappointed in the United States Supreme Court, and so is our great country!

💬 89.1K   ↻ 87K   ♡ 430.4K   ⬆️

Donald J. Trump ✔ @realDonaldTrump · Dec 19, 2020

Peter Navarro releases 36-page report alleging election fraud 'more than sufficient' to swing victory to Trump washex.am/3nwaBCe. A great report by Peter. Statistically impossible to have lost the 2020 Election. Big protest in D.C. on January 6th. Be there, will be wild!

ⓘ This claim about election fraud is disputed

Peter Navarro releases 36-page report alleging election fraud 'more tha...
Director of the Office of Trade and Manufacturing Policy Peter Navarro published a lengthy report Thursday outlining several examples of votin...
🔗 washingtonexaminer.com

💬 31.3K   ↻ 74.3K   ♡ 214.7K   ↑

Donald J. Trump ✔ @realDonaldTrump · Dec 20, 2020

GREATEST ELECTION FRAUD IN THE HISTORY OF OUR COUNTRY!!!

ⓘ This claim about election fraud is disputed

💬 63.4K   ↻ 94.8K   ♡ 416.3K   ↑

Donald J. Trump ✔ @realDonaldTrump · Dec 22, 2020

THE DEMOCRATS DUMPED HUNDREDS OF THOUSANDS OF BALLOTS IN THE SWING STATES LATE IN THE EVENING. IT WAS A RIGGED ELECTION!!!

ⓘ This claim about election fraud is disputed

💬 102.6K   ↻ 103.7K   ♡ 396.7K   ↑

Donald J. Trump ✓ @realDonaldTrump · Dec 24, 2020

VOTER FRAUD IS NOT A CONSPIRACY THEORY, IT IS A FACT!!!

(!) This claim about election fraud is disputed

💬 65.7K 🔁 120.4K ♡ 478.9K ⬆

Donald J. Trump ✓ @realDonaldTrump · Dec 24, 2020

Twitter is going wild with their flags, trying hard to suppress even the truth. Just shows how dangerous they are, purposely stifling free speech. Very dangerous for our Country. Does Congress know that this is how Communism starts? Cancel Culture at its worst. End Section 230!

💬 46K 🔁 96.3K ♡ 338.6K ⬆

Donald J. Trump ✓ @realDonaldTrump · Dec 25, 2020

MERRY CHRISTMAS!

💬 108.6K 🔁 116.9K ♡ 823.7K ⬆

Donald J. Trump ✓ @realDonaldTrump · Dec 26, 2020

I simply want to get our great people $2000, rather than the measly $600 that is now in the bill. Also, stop the billions of dollars in "pork".

💬 43.6K 🔁 81.6K ♡ 405.9K ⬆

Donald J. Trump ✓ @realDonaldTrump · Dec 30, 2020

JANUARY SIXTH, SEE YOU IN DC!

💬 46.8K 🔁 118.3K ♡ 457.5K ⬆

Donald J. Trump ✓ @realDonaldTrump · Dec 30, 2020

Twitter is shadow banning like never before. A disgrace that our weak and ineffective political leadership refuses to do anything about Big Tech. They're either afraid or stupid, nobody really knows!

💬 25.1K 🔁 68.4K ♡ 253K ⬆

Donald J. Trump ✓ @realDonaldTrump · Dec 30, 2020

The United States had more votes than it had people voting, by a lot. This travesty cannot be allowed to stand. It was a Rigged Election, one not even fit for third world countries!

(!) This claim about election fraud is disputed

💬 33.2K 🔁 79K ♡ 275.4K ⬆

Donald J. Trump ✔ @realDonaldTrump · Dec 31, 2020 ooo

Finished off the year with the highest Stock Market in history. Setting records with your 401k's, just like I said you would. Congratulations to all!

💬 41K   🔁 64.5K   ♡ 372.6K   ↑

Donald J. Trump ✔ @realDonaldTrump · Jan 1, 2021 ooo

HAPPY NEW YEAR!

💬 74.5K   🔁 90.2K   ♡ 679.6K   ↑

Donald J. Trump ✔ @realDonaldTrump · Jan 2, 2021 ooo

TRANSPARENCY in medical pricing will be one of the biggest and most important things done for the American citizen. It was just put into service, January 1, against long odds and bitter opposition. Final lawsuits won last week. Enjoy all the extra money you will have!

💬 14K   🔁 51.6K   ♡ 230.9K   ↑

Donald J. Trump ✔ @realDonaldTrump · Jan 2, 2021 ooo

MAKE AMERICA GREAT AGAIN!

💬 66.8K   🔁 93.4K   ♡ 533.5K   ↑

Donald J. Trump ✔ @realDonaldTrump · Jan 2, 2021 ooo

An attempt to steal a landslide win. Can't let it happen!

⚠ Election officials have certified Joe Biden as the winner of the U.S. Presidential election

> 🔵 **Senator Ted Cruz** ✔ @SenTedCruz · Jan 2, 2021
>
> .@AP: Cruz Leads 11 GOP Senators Challenging Biden Win Over Trump
> nbcconnecticut.com/news/politics/...

💬 22.7K   🔁 46.6K   ♡ 172.2K   ↑

Donald J. Trump ✔ @realDonaldTrump · Jan 3, 2021 ooo

The Swing States did not even come close to following the dictates of their State Legislatures. These States "election laws" were made up by local judges & politicians, not by their Legislatures, & are therefore, before even getting to irregularities & fraud, UNCONSTITUTIONAL!

⚠ This claim about election fraud is disputed

💬 24.6K   🔁 60.9K   ♡ 214.1K   ↑

Donald J. Trump ✓ @realDonaldTrump · Jan 5, 2021

The Vice President has the power to reject fraudulently chosen electors.

💬 101.4K   🔁 111.4K   ♡ 431.4K   ⬆️

Donald J. Trump ✓ @realDonaldTrump · Jan 5, 2021

Antifa is a Terrorist Organization, stay out of Washington. Law enforcement is watching you very closely! @DeptofDefense @TheJusticeDept @DHSgov @DHS_Wolf @SecBernhardt @SecretService @FBI

💬 37.8K   🔁 78.8K   ♡ 273.5K   ⬆️

Donald J. Trump ✓ @realDonaldTrump · Jan 6, 2021

If Vice President @Mike_Pence comes through for us, we will win the Presidency. Many States want to decertify the mistake they made in certifying incorrect & even fraudulent numbers in a process NOT approved by their State Legislatures (which it must be). Mike can send it back!

⚠️ This claim about election fraud is disputed

💬 78.8K   🔁 81.2K   ♡ 288.8K   ⬆️

Donald J. Trump ✓ @realDonaldTrump · Jan 6, 2021

States want to correct their votes, which they now know were based on irregularities and fraud, plus corrupt process never received legislative approval. All Mike Pence has to do is send them back to the States, AND WE WIN. Do it Mike, this is a time for extreme courage!

⚠️ This claim about election fraud is disputed

💬 33K   🔁 70.3K   ♡ 251.7K   ⬆️

Donald J. Trump ✓ @realDonaldTrump · Jan 6, 2021

THE REPUBLICAN PARTY AND, MORE IMPORTANTLY, OUR COUNTRY, NEEDS THE PRESIDENCY MORE THAN EVER BEFORE - THE POWER OF THE VETO. STAY STRONG!

💬 52.7K   🔁 73.8K   ♡ 344.5K   ⬆️

Donald J. Trump ✓ @realDonaldTrump · Jan 6, 2021

Even Mexico uses Voter I.D.

💬 55.1K   🔁 87.2K   ♡ 456.9K   ⬆️

Donald J. Trump ✔ @realDonaldTrump · Jan 6, 2021 ⠐⠐⠐

Mike Pence didn't have the courage to do what should have been done to protect our Country and our Constitution, giving States a chance to certify a corrected set of facts, not the fraudulent or inaccurate ones which they were asked to previously certify. USA demands the truth!

🗨   ⟲   ♡   ↑

Donald J. Trump ✔ @realDonaldTrump · Jan 6, 2021 ⠐⠐⠐

Please support our Capitol Police and Law Enforcement. They are truly on the side of our Country. Stay peaceful!

🗨 211.5K   ⟲ 150K   ♡ 582.6K   ↑

Donald J. Trump ✔ @realDonaldTrump · Jan 6, 2021 ⠐⠐⠐

I am asking for everyone at the U.S. Capitol to remain peaceful. No violence! Remember, WE are the Party of Law & Order – respect the Law and our great men and women in Blue. Thank you!

🗨 429K   ⟲ 222K   ♡ 727.4K   ↑

Donald J. Trump ✔ @realDonaldTrump · Jan 6, 2021 ⠐⠐⠐

These are the things and events that happen when a sacred landslide election victory is so unceremoniously & viciously stripped away from great patriots who have been badly & unfairly treated for so long. Go home with love & in peace. Remember this day forever!

🗨   ⟲   ♡   ↑

Donald J. Trump ✔ @realDonaldTrump · Jan 8, 2021 ⠐⠐⠐

The 75,000,000 great American Patriots who voted for me, AMERICA FIRST, and MAKE AMERICA GREAT AGAIN, will have a GIANT VOICE long into the future. They will not be disrespected or treated unfairly in any way, shape or form!!!

🗨 151.6K   ⟲ 137.6K   ♡ 482.5K   ↑

Donald J. Trump ✔ @realDonaldTrump · Jan 8, 2021 ⠐⠐⠐

To all of those who have asked, I will not be going to the Inauguration on January 20th.

🗨 304.4K   ⟲ 174.8K   ♡ 516.5K   ↑

President Trump ✔ @POTUS · Jan 9, 2021

🏳 US government account

As I have been saying for a long time, Twitter has gone further and further in banning free speech, and tonight, Twitter employees have coordinated with the Democrats and the Radical Left in removing my account from their platform, to silence me — and YOU, the 75,000,000 great...

💬   ↻   ♡   ⬆

President Trump ✔ @POTUS · Jan 9, 2021

🏳 US government account

...patriots who voted for me. Twitter may be a private company, but without the government's gift of Section 230 they would not exist for long. I predicted this would happen. We have been negotiating with various other sites, and will have a big announcement soon, while we...

💬   ↻   ♡   ⬆

President Trump ✔ @POTUS · Jan 9, 2021

🏳 US government account

...also look at the possibilities of building out our own platform in the near future. We will not be SILENCED! Twitter is not about FREE SPEECH. They are all about promoting a Radical Left platform where some of the most vicious people in the world are allowed to speak freely...

💬   ↻   ♡   ⬆

President Trump ✔ @POTUS · Jan 9, 2021

🏳 US government account

...STAY TUNED!

💬   ↻   ♡   ⬆

Printed in Great Britain
by Amazon

73536825R00076